BRANKO MITROVIĆ

T0272285

ARCHITECTURAL PRINCIPLES IN THE AGE OF FRAUD

WHY SO MANY ARCHITECTS PRETEND TO BE PHILOSOPHERS AND DON'T CARE HOW BUILDINGS LOOK

EDITIONS

ORO Editions
Publishers of Architecture, Art, and Design
Gordon Goff: Publisher

www.oroeditions.com
info@oroeditions.com

Published by ORO Editions

Author: Branko Mitrović
Book Design: Ahankara Art
Project Coordinator: Alejandro Guzman-Avila
Managing Editor: Jake Anderson

0 9 8 7 6 5 4 3 2 1 First Edition

ISBN: 978-1-954081-45-1

Color Separations and Printing: ORO Group Ltd.

Printed in China.

ORO Editions makes a continuous effort to minimize the overall carbon footprint of its publications. As part of this goal, ORO Editions, in association with Global ReLeaf, arranges to plant trees to replace those used in the manufacturing of the paper produced for its books. Global ReLeaf is an international campaign run by American Forests, one of the world's oldest nonprofit conservation organizations. Global ReLeaf is American Forests' education and action program that helps individuals, organizations, agencies, and corporations improve the local and global environment by planting and caring for trees.

In memoriam
Thomas Gordon Smith

CONTENTS

PREFACE
WHERE THINGS ARE GOING 7

INTRODUCTION
ARCHITECTURE, PHILOSOPHY
AND THE OBFUSCATORY TURN............ 9

CHAPTER 1
MODERNISM 16

CHAPTER 2
PHENOMENOLOGY 45

CHAPTER 3
DECONSTRUCTION 71

CHAPTER 4
THE ABYSS 101

CONCLUSION
BEYOND SALVAGE? 120

ENDNOTES 138

BIBLIOGRAPHY 152

INDEX 159

WHERE THINGS ARE GOING

Most readers of this book have probably experienced situations when someone enthusiastically talks nonsense to them, with great self-confidence, and also expects appreciation, or even admiration, for what is being said. (Having worked in architectural academia for a quarter of a century, I can testify how pervasive these situations can be). When one points out that what has been said is false, self-contradictory, maybe even unethical or stands for evil political views, the person smiles stupidly and responds by saying: "Yes, but that is where things are going." The response—one can hardly fail to notice—constitutes a clear admission of the lack of personal and intellectual integrity. By saying it, the person admits that his or her views, decisions, and actions are not his or her own, but result from an effort to be in line with "where things are going." It becomes hard to avoid the impression that this chatty conversationalist would have supported the Bolsheviks in Russia in 1917, Nazis in Germany in 1933 and would have been a vehement advocate of McCarthyism in the USA in the early 1950s. Arguably, someone who yields to social trends in a modern democratic society would be even more likely to do so in a system dominated by strong political pressures. In such conversations, my experience tells me, it helps little to point out that what is good or bad, true or false, has nothing to do with "where things are going." Attempts to explain this are typically met with more stupid smiles and polite evasion in the form of the statement "I am more interested to hear what you think about it." A change of the topic of conversation quickly follows.

This same lack of integrity, I argue in this book, stands behind the greatest predicament of architecture of our time. Architecture as a profession, and the architectural academia that trains architects, can hardly be said to enjoy much respect today. In fact, it is hard to think of an era when they were less valued. Prize-winning architectural works are often appreciated only by other architects. The general public ignores them or occasionally reacts against them with hostility. The widespread impression is that architects and architecture academics talk an incomprehensible jargon and design buildings that only they (say to) like. This use of incomprehensible jargon by architects and academics as well as the misemployment of philosophy on which it typically relies, is precisely the topic of this book. The fact that I work, research, and publish in both architecture and philosophy, and have formal qualifications in both fields, has naturally made me sensitive to architects' and architectural academics' (ab)use of philosophy. For many years I have collected examples of the misemployment of philosophical ideas, theories and concepts, in which architects and architectural academics have engaged, often without much understanding, in order to promote their careers, advocate and defend fashionable trends and impress and bamboozle colleagues and critics. By this time I have a substantial number of observations to tell about this phenomenon. I can even explain how it came about. The story that the book recounts is, I believe, often entertaining on the surface, but it is hard to deny that the wider picture the book presents is nothing short of depressing.

I promised to Thomas Gordon Smith that I would write this book decades ago. The project has always been on my mind but it has also taken a very long time to mature. In March 2020 the coronavirus pandemic interrupted my sabbatical at the University of Pennsylvania and forced me to return home to Norway. Even interlibrary loans were interrupted at the time and it was impossible to continue work on my current project about Guarino Guarini. At the same time, isolation enabled me to write this book, after many years that I have been planning it. I am exceptionally grateful to my former students Mark Gage and Cameron Moore for the extensive help, advice, and suggestions in the critical moments of the writing of the book. Regular discussions with my current doctoral students Amund Rolfsen and Øystein Holdø have provided stimulating thoughts and helped me formulate my ideas more clearly. Without the help of Astrid Sandvik and Stine Thordarson Moltubakk, librarians at my home institution, NTNU, it is hard to imagine that I would have been able to complete the book. The views on which this book relies were formed through my discussions and exchanges, agreements and disagreements with numerous colleagues and students over decades. It summarizes large part of my biography for the past quarter of the century to mention their names and express my gratitude in the order I got to know them: Samir Younés, Duncan Stroik, Tony van Raat, Wouter Boer, Damon Brider, Peter McPherson, Nick Zangwill, Michael Austin, David Chaplin, Renata Jadrašin-Milić and Ian Verstegen.

ARCHITECTURE, PHILOSOPHY AND THE OBFUSCATORY TURN

> *... and thou shalt have no other gods but these three: Chaos, Clouds and Blabbering.*
>
> *Aristophanes*[1]

The dominant role that obfuscation and philosophical posturing came to play in architectural discussions and writings during the twentieth century is one of the least studied aspects of the revolutionary changes that have shaken architecture for the past hundred years. The phenomenon became particularly vehement in the final decades of the last century, and it is fully appropriate to talk about the Obfuscatory Turn in architectural thinking during the era. This book is an attempt to contribute to the examination of this phenomenon, its manifestations and origins. Its aim is to describe and analyze the ways in which architects and architectural academics misemployed philosophy, philosophical works and philosophical arguments in order to advocate their approaches to architectural design. By "misemployment" I mean efforts that clearly indicate the poor understanding of philosophical sources, the miscomprehension of the arguments or conceptual distinctions on which they rely, the use of philosophical terminology without content or straightforward attempts to bamboozle readers, colleagues and the general public with philosophical terminology. These tendencies, I argue, are not mere incidents—rather, in important ways, they are constitutive of the profession that we call "architecture" today. They reflect many (prominent) architects' efforts to restructure the profession and its aims in accordance with their career aims, commercial and psychological needs, often in opposition to the interests of their clients or the general public, or even the long-term interests of their profession itself. While the resulting depiction

INTRODUCTION

hardly gives reasons for enthusiasm about the world of contemporary architecture, one should not forget that during the same period other fields of the humanities have also suffered from similar phenomena. Architecture cannot be exempted from general trends dominant in a society.

The origins of the phenomenon go back at least to the 1920s and the theoretical positioning of the protagonists of the nascent modernist movement. This is the topic of the first chapter of this book. Modernist architects turned to the German philosophy of history in order justify their core claim that architecture should be appropriate to its time. This claim was vital for modernists in order to dismiss alternative approaches to design, such as Classicism or neo-Gothic architecture. Theories about the spirit of the time, *Zeitgeist*, on which modernist architects such as Walter Gropius or Ludwig Mies van der Rohe relied were part of the belief, dominant in the German cultural context of the era, that spirits of collective entities such as epochs, eras, cultures, nations, races and similar determine the creativity of individuals who belong to these collectives.[2] (We shall see that modernists outside Germany accepted this assumption only with some delay.) The major problem with this view, that the proponents of modernist architecture simply decided to overlook, was that faith in such spiritual substances was incompatible with the materialist worldview based on modern science. Modernists' Modernism was, one could thus say, anti-modern in its core assumptions. Modern scientific worldview has nothing to say about spiritual forces that belong to eras, historical or social contexts.* It was precisely because

---

* This modern, materialist, perspective could be, for instance, the view that the mental states, the decisions or the creativity of historical figures, including architects, are biological phenomena, that biological phenomena are chemical and that chemical states ultimately result from interactions between physical particles. On this account, social influences (economy, tradition, style, fashion) can spread only by means that can have a physical description, such as interactions between individuals. Consequently, even if the majority of architects design in the same style during an era, one cannot say that that style is exclusively appropriate for the time. Simply, there is no force that would underwrite the claim that a specific style is exclusively appropriate for an era. If someone makes such a claim, this can only mean that he or she associates a certain style with the given era. This leaves architects free to design in the style that they and their clients prefer. If they design in a style that one does not associate with their era, one needs to revise one's associations and not to condemn architects.

they subscribed to anti-modern intellectual agendas and opposed the materialist perspectives of modern science that German philosophers or historians of the era advocated the view that spirits and communal substances exercise causal impact on history. This paradox about the anti-modern nature of the ideology of architectural Modernism illustrates a common characteristic of architects' engagements with philosophy. It reflects a pattern that we shall see repeated over and over again through the book. Often, the main reason why architects engage with works of philosophers is to utilize them as support for their own agendas. Their aim is not to achieve new insights. They do not seek to develop further or apply theories of philosophers. It would also be quite wrong to expect that they derive their approaches to design or architectural agendas from the philosophical positions they claim to endorse. Rather, for the past century philosophy has been used by architects mainly in order to legitimize their design agendas. These design agendas do not necessarily have much to do with the philosophical positions that architects invoke in order to justify them. It should therefore not be surprising that in the 1970s, when the failure of modernist architecture came to be openly recognized, its theoretical or philosophical deficiencies hardly ever came to be discussed. Nobody blamed German philosophers or historians for its failure. No effort was made to establish the theoretical errors that produced the aesthetic inadequacies of Modernism.

The 1970s are particularly important for our discussion here since this was the decade when the aesthetic failure of modernist architecture became obvious to the general public. Comparisons of newly-built hectares of glass boxes and concrete bunkers with older architecture became increasingly painful. During that decade, the rift between architects and the general public was sealed and it has never healed till our present day. Even those who believed that architecture should express its time ought to have found it difficult to believe that an architecture so unloved in its time can be its time's authentic expression. Tom Wolfe's *From Bauhaus to our House* is just one of many books that address the phenomenon. Today, there are web-pages and social media groups created specifically as a result of non-architects' efforts to understand the reasons for the ugliness of modernist architecture. At the moment I am writing these lines, a simple internet search that combines words "modern architecture" and "ugly" gives about 2.5 million sites where this combination of words occurs.

For our discussion here it is significant that the massive rejection of modernist architecture by the general public coincides in time, and I will argue in this book that it explains, another phenomenon: the rise of the Obfuscatory Turn. It was in the 1970s that architects and architectural academics massively started using obfuscation in their writings and discussions. Nothing similar can be found in the preceding decades of modernist optimism. Inept attempts to philosophize suddenly started to dominate architectural theory precisely in the moment when architects and academics would have been expected to articulate a clear response to the failure of the modernist project. This cannot be an accidental coincidence. For reasons explained later in the book, architects as a profession had no other choice but to continue to design modernist architecture even after its aesthetic deficiencies became widely recognized. Stylistic variations that have been introduced in later decades, until our present time, do not fundamentally depart from the same modernist paradigm. Similarly, architectural academics could not simply stop to teach Modernism. All other alternatives would have required exceptional efforts, fundamental re-training and force individuals who would take that path to swim against the current. The rise of the Obfuscatory Turn in such circumstances has to be understood as a desperate effort to justify the commitment to a paradigm that has failed and everyone knows about it. It is a strategy of denial. This is a very important point that this book seeks to make. A critic of contemporary architecture may get the impression that architects read books by some strange philosophers, get influenced by their ideas and then design the way they do. This is certainly wrong. Architects design the way they can, the way they know, and the way they have been taught. They are typically very cautious about their reputation and scared to do something that the rest of their profession would not approve of. Even today, it takes a lot of courage for an architect to step out of the modernist paradigm. In order to justify their designs, and in the situation when the general public often hates their work, they use words, phrases and ideas that they mine from books written by philosophers. Many academics base their careers on the fabrication of texts that use philosophical jargon in order to defend an approach to design that is hugely unpopular outside the architectural profession and academia. As for the understanding of or serious engagement with philosophical ideas, we shall see that it typically does not go very far.

Two core streams of the Obfuscatory Turn, "Phenomenology" and "Deconstruction" are discussed in the second and the third chapter.[3] Phenomenology is normally taken to include all those positions that put blame for the failure of Modernism on technology, the scientific worldview and rationality in general. The visual-aesthetic inadequacy of modernist architecture that the general public protests against is typically dismissed as an irrelevant concern, because visual perception is said to be always dependent on meanings, stories and narratives associated with architectural works. In other words, it does not matter how the building looks but what kind of story the architect can tell about it. Alternatively, it is claimed that concerns about the visual properties of buildings should be dismissed or not regarded as any more important than the way a building is experienced by other senses, the way it smells or even tastes. (In the second chapter we shall actually have to discuss the claim that the scale of a building can be established on the basis of how it tastes.) The alternative, deconstructivist approach sought to present a response to the critique of Modernism by relying on social Constructionism and anti-realism that were popular and influential in the final decades of the twentieth century. This was the idea that reality is merely constructed by forces such as language, culture, history, the social context or similar. Since human individuals and their biology on this account are social constructs too, traditional architectural concerns such as function, scale, relationship to the site and similar lose any relevance. Neither Phenomenology nor Deconstruction promoted a significant departure from modernist design practices. They have made no effort to address formal and visual-aesthetic deficiencies of Modernism. Rather, they provided the consolidation and defense of essentially modernist approaches to design under different names. Our topic here is the role that the Obfuscatory Turn and the (mis)use of philosophical ideas and jargon played in the formulation of these efforts. The second and the third chapter therefore aim to present a systematic survey of obfuscatory techniques and their typology. While architectural phenomenologists and deconstructivists relied on the same pool of obfuscatory techniques, their use was affected by the philosophical traditions they sought to emulate. We shall also see how these obfuscatory techniques were used in order to suppress concerns about the visual and formal-aesthetic qualities of architectural works.

The Obfuscatory Turn could have provided the justification of modernist designs only as long as recent philosophical production supplied philosophical works that could be mined for words, phrases and ideas. For almost three decades it was continental European, mainly German and French, philosophical works that were in the center of attention. This was natural because the alternative, English-speaking analytic philosophy was simply not suitable for the purpose. Analytic philosophers emphasize clarity and rigorous arguments in their writings. Their writings are often highly technical. Consequently, they provide limited material for the kind of reading that concentrates on mining philosophical texts for words, phrases and unusual claims. Probably for this same reason, continental philosophy came to exercise such a wide influence on the humanities departments at English-speaking universities since the 1970s. At the same time, it was never well received in English-speaking philosophy departments, where analytic philosophy reigned supreme. By the 1990s, however, continental philosophy was on its last breath. Younger generations of European philosophers increasingly turned to analytic philosophy. Philosophy departments at European universities eventually came to be predominantly staffed with analytic philosophers. This revolution in the philosophical culture on the European continent precipitated the crisis and ultimately the downfall of the Obfuscatory Turn in architecture. By the late 1990s it was becoming impossible to identify the new generation of prominent continental philosophers whose writings architects could exploit in order to legitimize their designs. Chapter Four describes the reactions to this crisis and the attempts that were made to overcome it. The crisis was additionally complicated by the fact that both the architectural profession and architectural academia faced the introduction of digital media during the same period. Finally, in the most recent decade, Object Oriented Ontology has provided a genuine philosophical perspective on architectural theory that avoids obfuscation. It has been largely endorsed as a reaction against social Constructionism ("Correlationism") that dominated architectural theory in the preceding decades. However, it has failed provide successful methods to theorize visual and formal-aesthetic issues in architectural design.

Philosophical posturing and the use of obfuscation in order to defend an unpopular architectural style can hardly suggest a favorable perspective on contemporary architectural profession and academia. The fact that these reactions were particularly widespread among architectural academics, who should have known better, is additionally depressing. Obviously, no historian can enter the minds and thoughts of the authors he or she is writing about or claim to be able to reconstruct their intentions. Also, people often act spontaneously and unconsciously when they defend and promote their interests. Authors that I write about in this book need not have employed obfuscation with conscious or malicious intentions. At most, one can point out when intellectual and theoretical positions coincide with commercial and career interests of their protagonists. This is certainly a relevant point to make when these positions are otherwise counterintuitive and their endorsement cannot be explained by some other motivation. A historian must always analyze not only what statements and documents assert, but also what they deny or conceal.

One may be tempted to compare this book with Alan Sokal's and Jean Bricmont's book *Fashionable Nonsense*. Sokal and Bricmont there collected and analyzed the false claims about physics and mathematics that prominent French post-modernists made in order to impress (or bamboozle) their readers. They were, however, dealing with a limited number of authors and a limited number of examples. In the case of architectural academia, the impact of the Obfuscatory Turn was so massive that any attempt to provide a comprehensive survey would take many thick volumes and many years of work. While working on this book I have had to limit my presentation to the most influential authors and seek the best examples of philosophical obfuscation and misunderstanding. Reading through the immense amount of meaningless texts that imitate philosophical jargon and that architectural academics produced in the 1980s and the 1990s in desperate attempts to improve their academic standing and show that they belong to the avant-garde is one of the most uninviting research projects one can imagine. It is also thoroughly depressing to think that these academics were doing the right thing insofar as they wanted to get prestigious jobs. They had no choice. One may have sympathy for them, but one should not forget that they have educated the architects who now build the environment we have to live in.

MODERNISM

"An evil fate wills it," Leibniz lamented once, "that men from time to time revert to darkness out of boredom with light."[4] Unlike earthquakes or epidemics, such events result from human will and actions. Individuals who foresee them may even try to prevent the disaster by arguing against the misconceptions that are about to cause it. Their reasoning may be solid, but as it is directed against the desires and fancies of the popular opinion, it necessarily fails to achieve its purpose. Arguably, this is what happened with Geoffrey Scott's book *The Architecture of Humanism*, at least in the eyes of those who regard the rise of modernist architecture as a major calamity of the modern era.[5] Written in the second decade of the twentieth century, Scott's book targeted a series of views about architecture ("fallacies" as he called them) that were increasingly becoming influential in his time. As it turned out, these same "fallacies" came to constitute the fundamental tenets of the modernist movement in the years after the first world war. Scott was, one could say, an anti-modernist before there was Modernism at all. At the same time, he was decidedly *modern* in the sense of the full endorsement of the modern scientific, materialist, worldview. Even from the perspective of our present-day physicalism—the view that everything is physical, that mental phenomena are ultimately reducible to neurobiology, biology to chemistry and chemistry to physics—Scott's perspectives on architectural theory can be seen as uncontroversial.

The most significant of the "fallacies" that Scott targeted is the attitude that he called "romantic": the view that evaluates all architectural works on the basis of the ideas associated with them. This is an approach that dismisses as insignificant the aesthetic qualities that arise purely from visual and formal elements (such as shapes or colors) or their combinations.[6] Instead, the "romantic fallacy" assumes that what matters in the works of art and architecture always depends on the meanings, ideas and concepts associated with these works. In opposition to the "romantic fallacy," Scott insisted that forms "impose their own aesthetic character on a dully sensitive attention, quite independently of what we may know, or not know about them."[7] The remaining "fallacies" that he described are variations of this "romantic" rejection of visual, formal-aesthetic concerns. They similarly seek to suppress interest in shapes and colors by emphasizing the ideas associated with architectural works. The "mechanical fallacy" is thus the view that our knowledge of the structure of a building modifies our aesthetic reaction. The "ethical fallacy" seeks to replace aesthetic evaluation with the ethical one. The "biological fallacy" consists in the evaluation of architectural works in relation to their position in a pre-conceived scheme of history, their appropriateness to (one's ideas about) their time.[8]

At the time Scott wrote his book, his opposition to the "romantic fallacy" reaffirmed an old formalist tradition. Early in the Renaissance Leon Battista Alberti defined beauty in a way that depends purely on shapes and is independent of associations one has with beautiful objects.[9] The same view—that beauty results from the relationship between visual, formal parts (and not from associations one may have with architectural works)—was repeated by other prominent authors during the Renaissance and Baroque eras such as Andrea Palladio or Guarino Guarini.[10] Scott's own formulations of aesthetic formalism in architecture relied on Immanuel Kant's aesthetic theories.[11] At the time he wrote, aesthetic formalism was thus a well-established perspective in architectural theory. It also correlated with contemporary models of architectural education, that emphasized visuality, formal composition and demanded high-level graphical skills from students and future architects.

When modernists go marching on...

Our story necessarily starts with the modernist movement's rejection of these views in the early decades of the twentieth century. The formalist assumption that aesthetic values of architectural works can be independent of ideas associated with these works had to be unacceptable for modernists from the beginning. Modernism in architecture is precisely the view that architectural works are always to be evaluated in relation to the ideas one has about the time when they were built. In other words, that their aesthetic qualities depend on how they express their time. In line with this, writings of prominent modernists such as Mies van der Rohe and Walter Gropius are loaded with invectives against aesthetic formalism and (what they call) "aesthetic speculation" that they associated with the training practiced in the architectural academies of the era.[12] A survey of Mies's writings indicates that until 1930 he dismissed aesthetic concerns in principle.[13] In later years he would accept them, but under condition that they do not violate other, non-formal, concerns, such as appropriateness to time. In 1928 the modernist congress (CIAM) in La Sarraz criticized architectural academies for their aesthetic and formalistically-driven methods of architectural education.[14] About that same time, Hannes Meyer at the Bauhaus opposed the aesthetic attitude to building, Buckminster Fuller complained against the "aesthetic and ethic leech-hold upon pioneering productivity" while Adolf Behne advocated the rejection of formalism and aesthetic concerns.[15] Similar anti-aesthetic and anti-formalist sentiments can be traced back to the writings of the earliest advocates of Modernism in the years before the first world war, such as Hermann Muthesius, Hendrik Petrus Berlage or Otto Wagner.[16] The negative attitude towards aesthetic concerns affected all aspects of modernists' doctrines, including, for instance, their views on heritage preservation. The modernist movement's (CIAM's) "Charter of Athens" thus accepted that historical buildings may be preserved as "expressions of earlier forms of life" but not for their aesthetic value.[17] It explicitly warned against efforts to adjust aesthetically new parts of cities to the old ones. As late as the 1960s, and in line with such views, Gropius opposed attempts to preserve the ambient of the Park Avenue in New York and defended the destruction of the Pennsylvania Station.[18]

Modernists' rejection of aesthetic formalism thus resulted from the demand that architecture should be appropriate to its time and the assumption that architectural works cannot be evaluated independently of how they relate to the ideas one has about the time when they were built. This assumption was also the most significant characteristic of modernist architectural theory from its earliest days. In the years before the first world war both Wagner and Muthesius insisted that artists must represent their time and that art should correspond to its time.[19] After World War One, such claims were reiterated *ad nauseam*. Mies van der Rohe in his writings and interviews kept repeating that "it should be possible to sense the character of our time in our buildings," that architects "should express the time," that "architecture can only be the expression of its civilization," that "architecture belongs to certain epochs; it expresses the real essence of its times" or that his own intention was to express his time through his work.[20] In Gropius's writings one similarly reads that "good architecture must mirror the life of the time," that it should be "a true mirror of the life and social behavior of the period," that buildings should be designed "in unmistakable terms of our own period," that one should "select artistic means which best express the ideas and spiritual directions of our time" and so on.[21]

Such claims have been repeated so many times that they may sound obvious to many people, but they are easier to state than to explain, elaborate or defend. On closer consideration, it is far from clear how buildings can express their time, nor why they need to do it, nor what benefits are achieved when this is (supposedly) the case. To start with, the twentieth century was one of the worst centuries in human history. It was an era of world wars and concentration camps. It may be pointed out that architecture should seek to give hope to people and therefore it should precisely avoid expressing its time like a plague. Moving into the twenty-first century, it is similarly far from obvious how our contemporary buildings can express an era of global warming or corona virus pandemic, nor why they should do so, nor what is achieved when they do it, nor what is missed when they do not. There is no logical link between the characteristics of an era and the shapes the architects give to the buildings they design. It is certainly reasonable that the new technology of the era should affect how buildings are *built*. It is, however, far from clear what its *formal* impact might have to be. In spite of the claims made by twentieth-century modernists, it is impossible to deduce flat roofs, asymmetrical plans or the absence of ornamentation from the characteristics of the twentieth century as an era or its technology. These formal characteristics simply do not logically follow from historical events or social relations dominant during the century, or even the latest building technology of the era. Building technologies of the twentieth century did not necessarily imply the shapes that modernist architects advocated. New materials and technologies could have been also used, for instance, for the cheap mass production of traditional facade ornaments. In the preceding centuries it was expensive to produce in stone the ornaments of the classical orders (Doric, Ionic, Corinthian). Modern stone cutting technology made such ornaments much more affordable. Someone may therefore argue that our era of modern technology should be an era of mass-produced classical ornamentation. There is no reason why an enthusiast of classical architecture may not endorse the use of modern materials. He or she may even go so far as to advocate the use of painted polystyrene columns for the ornamentation of facades. Polystyrene is certainly a modern-era material. A proponent of polystyrene classicism may rightly point out that the era of twentieth-century technology would be better expressed by polystyrene classicism than by flat roofs. Flat roofs that do not leak would have been very difficult to make with twentieth-century technology. Polystyrene classical columns would have been much more in line with the technology available during the era.

At the same time, modernists' writings are replete with claims that judgments of architectural works should depend on how they express the technology of their time. This view is precisely what Scott described as the mechanical fallacy. One finds such statements, for instance, in the writings of Adolf Loos, Mies van der Rohe and Gropius.[22] It remains unexplained why some aesthetic qualities could not be attributed purely on the basis of shapes and colors and independently of the material the object is made of. Antonio Sant' Elia actually claimed that the calculation of the resistance of materials, the use of steel and reinforced concrete and modern scientific concepts are incompatible with the use of historical styles in ornamentation.[23] He never explained why the structural calculation of a traditionally ornamented building would be impossible. Another example of mechanical fallacy is the demand that architectural works should clearly show the material they are made of.[24] It is, however, far from obvious that architecture would be deprived of aesthetic qualities just because its surfaces hide the materials its walls are made of. One commonly attributes aesthetic qualities to many architectural works that hide their structural materials. It is unclear why inaccurate information about the material a building is made of needs to be detrimental for our attribution of aesthetic qualities to that building.

THE MODERNIST AGENDA

These discussions illustrate an important aspect of the writings of twentieth-century advocates of Modernism. Their authors never bothered to consider or respond to the counterarguments that were obvious and well-known at the time. The claims and arguments they made in their writings were clearly not meant to be challenged. Modernist theorizing about architecture did not operate in the form of a debate or a logical analysis. The failure to consider opposing or alternative views may seem to undermine its credibility, but this impression merely results from the inaccurate expectation that the claims and arguments stated by modernists were decisive for their endorsement of Modernism. In fact, arguments that were stated, were stated in order to justify a pre-determined design agenda. As we shall see later in this book, this design agenda itself was not endorsed because of the arguments that the advocates of Modernism stated. Modernists did not start to design the way they did because they were originally convinced by the arguments that one can read in their writings. Rather, they stated the arguments in order to justify and advocate their approach to design that they endorsed for other reasons. These are important observations for someone who seeks to understand what happened with architecture in the twentieth century. If the modernist agenda was not derived from the arguments that its protagonists state in their texts, then one has to inquire about the motivation that generated the agenda, made it credible and ultimately widely accepted. We shall come to analyze this motivation later in this book. At this stage it is important to clarify the architectural content of the agenda. From our contemporary perspective, the criteria by which individual buildings designed in the 1920s and the 1930s were classified as "modern"—that is, appropriate to the modern era—are not necessarily obvious. It is enough to compare buildings designed by Mies van der Rohe, Le Corbusier and Frank Lloyd Wright to see how difficult it is to specify what constitutes the formal language of modernist architecture. It is not easy to talk about the formal unity of the modernist style, the way this can be done in the case of Gothic or Renaissance architecture.

If one surveys the works and writings of the leading protagonists of the modernist movement, it is the rejection of ornamentation, and especially traditional approaches to ornamentation, that comes forward as the most significant common denominator. This is also further confirmed by the extremely negative and hostile reactions against those modernists who crossed the line and dared employ traditionally looking ornaments. This famously happened to Jacobus Oud or Edward Durrell Stone.[25] The preference for flat roofs and horizontal windows also seems to relate to the effort to reject the traditional appearance of buildings. (It is impossible to say that twentieth-century technology made pitched roofs and vertical windows obsolete or to deduce flat roofs and horizontal windows from the characteristics of the modern era or twentieth-century technology.)

The use of modern technology in itself could not be stated as the criterion to differentiate modernist buildings from those of non-modernist contemporary architects. Other contemporary architects—for instance, classicists such as John Russell Pope—were as modern in their use of technology as any modernists. Skyscrapers built in the USA before World War Two were typically covered with traditional and classical ornaments. There is thus no reason why classicists could not design skyscrapers, or use steel or concrete skeleton systems. For neo-Gothic architects such structural systems would have been in line with their tradition anyhow. An important difference, however, was the possibility of open plan that was enabled by skeleton structures. Traditional architectural training in early twentieth-century architectural academies emphasized the composition of enclosed spaces, their alignments and proportional adjustments. Wright complained that such composition, "since the Renaissance ... was all the method we had in Architecture."[26] The introduction of skeleton structure enabled modernists to abandon traditional spatial composition and introduce open plan. This was indeed an important difference. As Wright put it, "'Composition' in Architecture is, I hope, dead."[27] The rejection of symmetrical plans was a collateral result of the rejection of spatial composition. Asymmetrical plans on their own could not be an important element of differentiation from traditional designs of the era. Neo-Gothic architects had no reasons to hesitate to use asymmetrical plans. Also, residential buildings by Pope or McKim, Mead and White were often asymmetrical in plan. When it comes to façades, many important modernist works are symmetrical, including Le Corbusier's Villa Savoye to Mies's National Gallery in Berlin.

The core of the modernist agenda in architectural design were thus two major *negative* principles: the rejection of traditional methods of façade ornamentation and the rejection of spatial composition. It was precisely in these matters that modernists' approach to design was in sharp collision with the approaches taught at contemporary architectural academies. Academic training emphasized ornamentation and the composition of spaces. Modernists' attack on academies as the established institutions of architectural education needs to be understood in this context. CIAM's declaration from La Sarraz advocated the abolition of architectural academies as "defenders of the past."[28] Equivalent attacks on the training models of the era, because they emphasized training in traditional and classical ornamentation are to be found in the writings of, for instance, Sant' Elia, Le Corbusier or Gropius (who used the dismissive phrase "applied archaeology").[29]

The modernist agenda also included the ideological claim that only the buildings that reject traditional approaches to façade ornamentation and spatial composition are properly "modern." From this point of view, the buildings that do not confirm to the modernist design agenda are not *appropriate* for the modern era. It is further assumed that this inappropriateness to time is undesirable and that such buildings should not be designed or built. Theoretical writings of the advocates of Modernism never explain why. It should be, after all, legitimate for an architect to seek to produce works that are timeless, transcultural or multicultural, rather than contemporary or limited to only one cultural context. Such aspirations cannot be dismissed as unrealistic, since many architectural works from the past are appreciated today, which suggests that some architectural values can be trans-cultural. Without argument one cannot simply assume that timeless architectural values are impossible, or that all architectural values are always relative to time.

Ghosts of history

The assumptions necessary in order to sustain claims about the exclusive appropriateness of modernist design to modern time were imported into architectural theory from German philosophy of history. Taken in its original meaning, the word "modern" simply means "contemporary." By definition, *every* architecture is modern at the time when it is built. "Modernist," however, as used through this book, implies the assumption that one can (and should) differentiate between architectural works that are "appropriate" or "inappropriate" for their time. This is the view that architecture can somehow belong or not belong to the time when it is built. Two buildings, from this point of view, can be built at the same time, and it may still happen that only one of them is "modern." It is further assumed that certain characteristics, such as the absence of ornamentation are particularly suited to modern era. The necessary background supposition is that there is an order in the history of human creativity. In other words, human history (and architectural history with it) is not merely a product of actions and interactions of large sets of human beings; historical developments do not result from independent decisions and actions of individuals. If this were the case, then historical developments would be haphazard and individual architects could decide whether they will design modernist-looking or neo-Gothic buildings. Interactions between individuals (such as artistic education) could make certain forms of design or styles widespread or even dominant in a given era, but this would not mean that there is something wrong with artists and architects who do not follow the same trends as the rest of their colleagues. Contrary to this view, in order to claim that some architectural styles are particularly suited to certain eras, modernists had to assume that history, including architectural history, is driven by a spiritual force that has the causal capacity to determine the actions of individuals and their creativity. Attempts to resist this force are pointless and considered as something bad. (The implicit idea is not only that one should always be on the winning side, but that the winner is always right, that there is no right or wrong, ugly or beautiful, beyond the dictates of the historical moment.) The proponents of this view preclude the possibility that an individual may be right when acting with integrity and in opposition to social trends. In their view, historical trends are always right and individuals (architects) should seek to be in line with them. In the modern era, this understanding of history has been a distinct characteristic of German cultural traditions.[30] For the past two-and-half centuries, German philosophers and historians have been inclined to postulate supra-individual spiritual forces that they believed determined the course of history. Through the twentieth century their views came to exercise a massive influence on the architectural and art theory.

The concept of *Zeitgeist*, the spirit of the time, associated with such conceptions of history, goes back to an eighteenth-century essay by Johann Gottfried Herder.[31] The form in which the idea came to influence twentieth-century architectural theory, however, originates from a rather vehement methodological debate between German historians that took place in the 1890s. The debate was triggered by Karl Lamprecht's efforts to replace historical explanations that relied on the decisions, actions and the creativity of individuals by explanations that relied on social factors.[32] Intellectual lives and the creativity of historical figures are, from this latter point of view, merely manifestations of the social and historical contexts they belong to.[33] Lamprecht assumed that by classifying actors into their historical contexts one can explain their actions and their creativity. The method, that came to dominate works of German historians in subsequent decades, postulated genuine causal capacities of social and historical contexts, eras and periods, over and above anything that results from the actions and interactions of the participating individuals. Lamprecht's critics did not fail to notice that his approach attributed to social and historical contexts the powers that some older historians attributed to God.[34] This is an important point: a religious worldview packaged into sociological terminology still remains a religious worldview. When modernists argued that it was wrong to design against the will of the *Zeitgeist*, this was not unlike the way followers of various religions believe that it is a sin to act against the will of God. The important difference is that for the followers of the Judeo-Christian-Islamic traditions, God's commandments do not change. For the architects who follow the commandments of *Zeitgeist* they change with time (and we shall also see that these changes conveniently happen in accordance with their own commercial and career interests). In the writings of art- and architectural historians of the decades preceding the first world war, one finds the same tendency to attribute divine-like causal capacities to historical and social contexts. The Viennese art historian Alois Riegl, for instance, postulated the Artistic Will of the community, *Kunstwollen*, as a self-propelled force that determines the artistic creativity of an era.[35] In his view, one and the same Artistic Will applies to the whole community. The artistic creativity of a community is then not a sum of creativities of individual artists, but a result of the communal Artistic Will that determines the creativity of individuals. Since differences between individuals are irrelevant, one can even attribute the views of an author to all other individuals who lived in the same era. All late Roman artists, he assumed, shared St Augustine's views about art even if they did not read him.[36] Riegl dismissed the criticism that different people from the same era may have different views as "materialist."[37] In his view, a spiritual force such as *Kunstwollen* determines the views of everyone living in the context.

In the years that followed the first world war, Oswald Spengler's *Decline of the West* significantly contributed to the popularization of the idea that creativity does not belong to individuals but to epochs. In Spengler's description, cultures such as Greco-Roman ("Apollonian") or modern western ("Faustian") repeat the same patterns of development. They also have their own specific identities. These identities are to be established using analogies. (We shall see that, following Spengler, some advocates of Modernism heavily relied on analogies in the decades that followed.) Spengler, for instance, claimed that in the western culture there exist deep analogies between the use of perspective in painting, the invention of book printing, the credit system and counterpoint in music. Similarly, he claimed that there were deep analogies between the naked statue, polis, and the Greek gold coin.[38] In his view the way cultures develop is fully predetermined by their identities. Consequently, actions and decisions of individuals play no role. Rather, the predetermined structures of cultural development ensure that events (including historical or artistic developments) happen the way they have to happen within the wider scheme of cultural history. In Spengler's view, had Napoleon died in some early battle of his career, another general would have taken his place and the history of Napoleonic would have happened the same way.[39]

Few historical books written in the twentieth century suffered so many utterly devastating reviews by professional historians as Spengler's *Decline of the West*.[40] Also, few exercised such a massive influence. Professional historians did all they could to distance themselves from the book in public, but contemporary German-speaking scholarship massively indulged in Spengler-style analogies in order to establish the spiritual characteristics of various eras. In art historians' writings one could witness the proliferation of efforts to establish similarities between, for instance, Vermeer's paintings and Spinoza's philosophy or between Gothic cathedrals and Scholasticism.[41] The faith that spiritual supra-individual forces determine the creativity of individuals came to dominate German scholarship in the first half of the twentieth century. As the art historian Dagobert Frey presented this view, the creative subject is to be conceived of as an ideal entity and not a biographical person; biographical persons (i.e. artists) are irrelevant in the study of artworks.[42] A good example of this approach is Wilhelm Worringer's claim to have discovered the influence of Hellenism on Japanese art.[43] Hellenism, he implied, is a spiritual substance that can overcome geographical distances, so it is irrelevant that there were no contacts between Japanese artists and artists of the Hellenistic era. The methodological approach taught to German art history students during the early decades of the twentieth century precisely consisted in seeking analogies in order to define the spirit of an era or a community. A good example is Robert Hedicke's 1924 methodology textbook for art history students.[44] According to Hedicke, art historians study the (artistic) manifestations of the Spirit

(*Geist*) in human cultures.[45] For instance, in order to understand Gothic art, one needs to grasp something that Hedicke calls Gothic spiritual totality.[46] The method they were taught, Gombrich observed many years later, made German art history students believe "that in the Gothic age Gothic cathedrals sprang up spontaneously all over Europe without any contact between the building sites."[47] In other words, it was understood that the Gothic Spirit simply imposed itself on different building sites over western Europe during the era. From this point of view, interactions between artists, including the training that individual architects or artists received or did not receive is irrelevant for their creativity. Presumably, architectural or art works would have come about in the form they did as a result of the spiritual intervention regardless of the capacities of individual artists. (This is not unlike Spengler's claim that Napoleonic wars would have happened the same way even had Napoleon died early in his career.) A good example of this reasoning one finds in the discussion of early Christian paintings in Roman catacombs by another Viennese art historian, Max Dvořák. Dvořák denied that the poor representational qualities of these paintings and the failure to represent objects in space derive from poor technical skills of the artists.[48] Rather, the spirit of the community determined their creativity in line with the historical developments of the era.

Architectural discussions in the early twentieth century cannot be understood independently of the influence that these ideas exercised on architects and architectural thinkers. Architects who were formed in the German cultural context were particularly exposed to views that attributed causal capacities to epochs, periods, and social contexts in general. This was reflected in their writings. Among the early advocates of Modernism, one finds this view stated as early as 1889 in a lecture by Berlage.[49] According to Erich Mendelsohn, the time itself has the power to determine artists' decisions.[50] Bruno Taut's view was that it is impossible to repeat old forms from the past.[51] In his writings from the 1920s, Mies van der Rohe insisted that ancient temples, Roman basilicas or medieval cathedrals were created by their epochs and were not works of individuals.[52] The individual, from his point of view, has no relevance.[53] Mies repeatedly stated that time is the supra-individual force that determines architectural production. The term *Zeitwille,* "the will of time," that he abundantly used in his writings clearly parallels Riegl's Artistic Will, *Kunstwollen.*[54] Historical buildings, he says, are bearers of the will of time.[55] The art of building, he also claimed, carries out spiritual decisions tied to time.[56] Similarly, Gropius referred to spiritual substances in order to advocate modernist architecture. Work in Bauhaus, he reports, was intended to make artistic creation "part of the development of a genuine *Zeitgeist*."[57]

MODERNISM WITHOUT SPIRITUALIST SUPERSTITIONS: IS IT EVEN POSSIBLE?

During the 1920s spiritualist conceptions of history still exercised a limited influence outside the German cultural realm. Having escaped the Third Reich, Nikolaus Pevsner complained in 1940 that the view that the essence of an era can be established by studying (Spengler-style) analogies was unknown to historians in England where he lived in exile.[58] Indeed, it was the wave of German-speaking academics-refugees from the 1930s that made spiritualist perspectives on history better known outside Germany. A good illustration is the problems Le Corbusier's faced when he sought to justify the concept of appropriateness to time in his writings from the early 1920s. In his *Toward an Architecture* (written in the early 1920s) Le Corbusier still seems not to have postulated a supra-individual spirit of time that rules over human affairs and determines human thoughts.[59] *Esprit*, "spirit," that he talked about in *Toward an Architecture* is shared by human individuals and does not have independent existence or causal capacities on its own. A systematic survey of his use of the term *esprit* through the book indicates that by this he meant the (widely shared) contents of mental states or attitudes of individuals. The term does not seem to refer to a spiritual substance over and above human individuals. One thus does not find in *Towards an Architecture* the kind of spiritualism that one encounters in the contemporary writings of Mies or Gropius. (It would be interesting if scholars specializing in Le Corbuser's work could establish when, in his later career, he began relying on the assumption that independently existing spiritual forces determine the course of history.) The important consequence was that in *Toward an Architecture* Le Corbusier could not easily make claims about the appropriateness of specific architectural forms to modern time. Without a supra-human force that drives human history, and underwrites such distinctions, we can merely say that some people think that some forms are more contemporary, while other people may disagree. The difficulty becomes obvious when Le Corbusier comes to praise the Parthenon in his book.[60] Insofar as the Parthenon can be appreciated from our modern perspective, it is hard to say why similar buildings should not be built again or its shapes replicated in the modern era. Le Corbusier's dismissal of Madeleine (a nineteenth-century church in Paris that resembles an ancient temple) only further weakens his position. He says that it "does not touch our axis" because of its imperfect detailing and the lack of proportional harmonies.[61] The explanation suggests that if buildings similar to the Parthenon were made today with proper detailing and proportional relationships they would be aesthetically as successful as the ancient one. This understanding is also strengthened by Le Corbusier's insistence that it is purely the forms of the Parthenon, not their symbolism (i.e ideas associated with these forms), that provoke "categorical emotions."[62] If it is purely the quality of shapes that matters, then well-detailed and proportioned buildings with classical ornamentation built today should be as good as any modernist building. The associations we may have about the time when they were built ought to be irrelevant.

Insofar as they avoided spiritualist assumptions, architectural historians writing about twentieth-century architecture inevitably struggled to explain the concept of "modern architecture." This is particularly obvious when one considers historical accounts of architecture built before World War Two. Before the 1940s modernist architecture was certainly not dominant, and its impact on the built environment was marginal. It is therefore hard to believe that no classicist or neo-Gothic structures built before 1940 are relevant or important enough to be mentioned or discussed in histories of twentieth-century architecture. Nevertheless, such buildings are almost utterly missing from numerous books that survey the topic. In a precocious display of cancel culture, generations of architectural historians seem to have sought to show that during the twentieth century no significant architecture was built outside the modernist paradigm. This applies even to books published decades after the modernist agenda ceased to be explicitly advocated by architects. The massive and lavishly illustrated *Architecture in the Twentieth Century* by Peter Gössel and Gabriele Leuthäuser published in 1990 simply leaves the works of major non-modernist architects such as John Russell Pope, McKim, Mead and White, Albert Speer, Armando Brasini, Edwin Lutyens or Ivan Zholtovsky unmentioned. They are also unmentioned in Reyner Banham's *Theory and Design in the First Machine Age*—a highly influential study that precisely concentrated on the architecture of the first four decades of the twentieth century.

Henry-Russell Hitchcock in his *Architecture: Nineteenth and Twentieth Centuries* openly admits that most architectural production before World War Two was a continuation of traditional approaches.[63] Nevertheless, his discussion of the architecture built according to the modernist paradigm during that period takes six times as much space in the book.[64] A similar phenomenon can be observed in numerous other books that pretend to survey architectural history of the last century. In the case of American architecture, the fact that the early decades of the last century were the golden era of American classicism has been a major problem for historians biased in favor of modernism. The widespread tendency to go silently over John Russell Pope's work is a particularly conspicuous example of ideologically bigoted history writing. Pope's contributions were decisive for the form of the Mall in Washington and it is inconceivable that he may be left unmentioned.[65] The decades preceding World War Two were the period when the Mall generally received its final shape. Architectural histories of the era that fail to discuss this massive project of monumental architecture (and they mostly do) are as convincing as attempts to write a history of Mediterranean architecture without mentioning the Roman forum.

Modernism's anti-modernity

It may seem that a way an architectural historian can avoid the need to discuss non-modernist architecture in the twentieth century is to talk about "modern" rather than "twentieth-century" architecture. Presumably, by using the former rather than the latter words in the title of a book an architectural historian can delimit the topic and thus avoid being dishonest about the book's content. The implicit assumption is that readers share with the author the same understanding about the meaning of the term "modern"—that they will agree about the kind of architecture that should count as "modern." As Charles Jencks put it, when one hears a historian say "Modern Movement" one should expect:

> some all-embracing theory, one or two lines of architectural development, something called 'the true style of our century', and a single melodrama with heroes and villains who perform their expected roles according to the historian's loaded script. Dazzled by the display a consistent and inexorable plot, the reader forgets to ask about all the missing actors and their

various feats—all that which ends up on the scrap of the historian's rejection pile.[66]

The problem is, however, that "modern" actually means "contemporary" and insofar as Wright counts as "modern" Pope must be "modern" too. It is unclear how one can declare one architect as "modern" and deny that status to another if they were both contemporaries. Jean-Louis Cohen in his book *The Future of Architecture* almost apologizes for using the term "modern classicism" because it is an "apparent oxymoron."[67] It is not clear why this should be the case— nor how buildings built in the modern era, classical or not, could not be "modern." The distinction cannot be made without the imposition of some additional belief about the "modern" buildings—typically, how "modern" buildings should look like. But then, if one is to claim that, for instance, modern buildings should be un-ornamented and have asymmetrical plans, one has to explain why this is so. It is not clear how one can justify this differentiation if one does not postulate a supra-human spiritual force that will decide which forms are appropriate and which are not. Without such a force one has to accept that there is nothing wrong if different architects follow different styles. Admittedly a small number of architects did choose to design buildings with asymmetrical plans and unornamented facades in the first half of the twentieth century. It is, however, impossible to state the reason why historians would privilege this marginal group in books that seek to provide a general survey of the architecture of the era. Modernism was not the dominant style of the era between the two world wars and it is utterly unclear why one should believe that only this particular style, marginal in this epoch, was the only appropriate one for the time. Generations of architectural historians who wrote on "modern architecture" and wanted to use their writings in order to assert their allegiance to Modernism struggled with this problem. Consider, for instance, Leonardo Benevolo's attempt to solve this problem in his *History of Modern Architecture* by saying that modern architecture was "born from the technical, social and cultural changes connected with the Industrial Revolution."[68] The obvious difficulty is that classical and neo-Gothic architects of the early twentieth century also relied on the benefits of the industrial revolution. It remains unclear why they should not count as "modern." The reader is ultimately left in the dark about the criteria that Benevolo used to differentiate between buildings which are modern and those which are not.

The complexity of the problem is best illustrated if we consider some of the strategies used in order to overcome it. One approach could be called "the heroic stance." In this case the historian simply denies the relevance of non-modernist architectural works built in the first four decades of the last century. J. M. Richards in his *Modern Architecture* describes that American architects trained at the *Beaux Arts* school in Paris "eclipsed their own masters in the inventiveness with which banks, libraries, and business houses were decked out with Florentine Renaissance detail."[69] He then concludes: "In the hands of such remarkable men as McKim, Mead, and White this sort of thing was done with astonishing facility; but this too, as we realize today, has little to do with architecture."[70] In other words, in his view, works such as McKim, Mead and White's Pennsylvania Station in New York or Pope's National Gallery in Washington simply do not count as architecture. An open admission of bias of this scale can only reflect the author's desperation and awareness of his inability to defend his position. Sometimes a heroic denial can result from the way an author structures the book or its chapters. In his *The Future of Architecture* Jean-Louis Cohen dedicates 183 pages to architecture between the two world wars, but only one 11-pages chapter to "classicisms and traditionalisms," as he puts it.[71] Even then, a substantial part of this only chapter about non-modernist architecture pertains to modernist works. The photograph of Gio Ponti's *modernist* building of the School of Mathematics in Rome is awarded two pages *in that same chapter*. One has to wonder why Gio Ponti's *modernist* work is given such a prominence while Armando Brasini's *classical* work is excluded from the discussion of *classical* architecture in Italy in the twentieth century.

An alternative approach consists of including pictures of a number of non-modernist buildings in order to dismiss them with disparaging comments. At the same time, the same features that are criticized in the non-modernist buildings are to be found in modernist works praised in the same book. Jürgen Joedicke in his *A History of Modern Architecture* thus presented a tiny picture of a New York skyscraper by Ernest R. Flagg from 1915 with a brief criticism "Lack of proportions, arbitrary mixture of styles (Renaissance and Baroque features piled one on the top of the another)."[72] However, "lack of proportion" could also be reproached to any other modernist skyscraper that he praises in his book. Also, Renaissance and Baroque features have been successfully combined in a single building many times through history. Joedicke similarly criticized Paul Ludwig Troost's House of German

Art by saying: "[l]ifeless rows of closely packed columns. Blank wall surfaces."[73] The criticism is grotesque, since *most* modernist buildings that he praises in his book actually have blank wall surfaces. Following the same criteria, it would be necessary to dismiss, for instance, Mies van der Rohe's Crown Hall on the IIT campus as a lifeless row of glass panels.[74] (Admittedly, it is hard to think of architectural works that are more lifeless than Miesian boxes.) William Curtis in his *Modern Architecture* dismissed Reginald Bloomfield's 1923 façades in Regent Street in London as "uninspired reworkings of motifs derived from Palladio and Sansovino."[75] In fact, the elements that come from Palladio or Sansovino in Bloomfield's rather Baroque-looking façades are hard to identify. More importantly, it is difficult to say that Bloomfield's façades are less inspired than the numerous concrete bunkers or glass boxes that Curtis praises in his book. Cohen, in the chapter mentioned above, brusquely dismissed Pope's National Gallery in Washington as "a Pantheon wrapped in a white stone sarcophagus."[76] The only similarities that Pope's building shares with the Pantheon are the dome and the portico. There are hundreds of classical buildings that have a dome and a portico and the association is arbitrary. The National Gallery, in fact, significantly differs from the Pantheon both in the composition of the space under the dome and the design of the portico.* The disparaging comparison of side wings with "a white stone sarcophagus" is unexplainable—Roman sarcophagi, for instance, were typically ornamented which is not the case with the walls of the National Gallery's side wings. The impression that Cohen is biased and unwilling to engage with the building he is writing about is hard to avoid.

ONLY GHOSTS COULD JUSTIFY MODERNISM! (BUT THERE AREN'T ANY.)

One could thus say that unrestrained bias in favor of the modernist movement often undermines the scholarly credibility of many works about the history of twentieth-century architecture. The major problem

---

* The dome of the National Gallery is supported by columns and the resulting space is very different from the one in the Pantheon. Columns of the portico of the National Gallery are Ionic as opposed to the Corinthian of the Pantheon's portico. Pantheon's pediment is notoriously steep whereas the pediment on the National Gallery is much more in line with the tradition. See also the discussion in the Conclusion of this book.

with many of these books is, however, not merely that they openly show bias but that they reek with desperation because of their inability to justify it. This negative judgment needs to be mitigated by the fact that their authors struggled with an irresolvable dilemma. Insofar as they did not rely on spiritual, supra-individual forces (such as *Zeitgeist*) that would underwrite the distinctions they wanted to make, it is not clear how they could say that some architectural works are proper for an era and others are not. Without a superior force that determines the direction in which history will or should develop, it becomes difficult to explain why architectural works with traditional ornaments and symmetrical plans are inappropriate for modern time and should be suppressed in historical works that survey the architecture of the era. More generally, the very concept of appropriateness to time becomes a distinction without a difference. It becomes impossible to argue that individual architects should not be allowed to decide freely about the style they want to use. In order to say that it is wrong—that it is a sin—to design a classical building in the modern era, one must postulate a spiritual force, something like a God of architectural styles, who decides which styles are sinful. Without such a superior force, it also becomes perfectly legitimate for architects and clients to have their own stylistic preferences. Nevertheless, the curious faith that the modernist approach to design is the only correct one in the modern era, without there being any historical force that would justify this claim on exclusivity, is remarkably entrenched. It is often expressed spontaneously by authors who endorse the modernist worldview. Greg Lynn, whose writings will be discussed later in this book, noted with surprise that the authors of the competition brief for the 1990s Cardiff Bay Opera House competition asked for a symmetrical horse-shoe plan of the opera hall.[77] He did not explain what kind of historical force he believed would prevent clients from preferring symmetrical plans in the modern era.

It is useful to compare these difficulties with the perspectives of those historians who openly relied on spiritual substances in order to justify their faith in Modernism. They solved the problem easily. As mentioned, Weimar-era approaches to historical scholarship trained students to search for analogies in order to discover and describe the impact of spiritual forces in history. Siegfried Giedion in his *Space, Time and Architecture* recounts how his studies taught him "to grasp the spirit of an epoch."[78] As described above, the method consisted in the search for analogies from which the historian would "infer" the nature of the spirit of the era. Giedion thus claims that the tendency of cubist painters to represent objects from different sides is "the artistic equivalent" of the views about space-time articulated in 1908 by the mathematician Hermann Minkowski.[79] Similarly, when Picasso and contemporary engineers arrive at similar forms, this means that "mechanical shapes and the shapes evolved by art as the mirror of a higher reality" rank as equivalent in terms of development.[80] Since Calculus was discovered during the Baroque era, Giedion claims that it "is a perfectly consistent outgrowth of the baroque universalistic point of view."[81] He proves that the spirit of the modern era favors modernist architecture by pointing out that Gropius used windows with a fixed glass panel in the middle without being aware that the same idea was also used by the Chicago school.[82] The background assumption is that the spirit of the era affected the design of windows at various geographical locations at the same time. It clearly parallels the belief of German art history students, reported by Gombrich, that Gothic cathedrals sprang all across western Europe without any contact between building sites. According to Giedion, the fundamental link between modern era engineering, art and architecture is in the use of empty, unornamented surfaces. The way the engineer Robert Maillart developed the slab into a basic element of construction, modern painters have made surface an essential factor in the composition of a picture.[83] This is a definite parallelism of methods, he claims: "a new method of construction found its simultaneous echo in a parallel method in art."[84] Spenglerian analogies of this kind thus enable Giedion to *deduce* the appropriateness of unornamented building surfaces to the modern era. As described above, such a deduction remained beyond reach for non-spiritualist modernist historians.

An approach similar to Giedion's, analyzed in a comprehensive study by David Watkin, can be found in Pevsner's writings.[85] Similarly to Spengler and Giedion, Pevsner stated that "Hobbes's and Spinoza's philosophy, Bernini's and Rembrandt's art, Richelieu's and Cromwell's statecraft have certain fundamentals in common, and on these we can establish a Baroque style of exact meaning."[86] Architecture, he says, is the product of "the changing spirits of changing ages. It is the spirit of an age that pervades its social life, its religion, its scholarship, and its arts."[87] A historian like himself, Pevsner confidently assumes, can recognize "the genuine and legitimate style of our [twentieth] century."[88] As we have seen, this is achieved through the study of analogies. It is important to bear in mind that these spirits cannot be mere metaphors for attitudes of individuals that were widespread during the era. If this were so, then claims about the appropriateness of styles to these eras could not be made. Rather, they have to be genuine supra-individual forces that are imagined to determine the (creative) attitudes of individuals, and decide which ones are proper for the time.

Faith in spirits of history, time, community and similar can thus produce miracles in discussions about Modernism. Without such faith it is not clear how one can say that some architectural works are appropriate to their time and others are not. Without the force that would underwrite order in history, it becomes impossible to differentiate between a modern and non-modern building in the case the two buildings are built at the same time. Obviously, this can hardly be an argument in favor of spiritualism. Rather, it points out to a serious problem for the theoretical justification of modernist architecture.

It is certainly paradoxical to preach the appropriateness of architecture to the modern era of science and technology and justify this concept of appropriateness by beliefs in spiritual forces that underwrite historical developments. The same applies if spiritual forces are not explicitly mentioned, but one adopts a position (such as the belief in order in history) that can be defended only by postulating them. Spiritualism is a distinctly non-modern assumption. It may not be clear how architecture can be appropriate to its time, but it should be clear that spiritualism is not compatible with the a worldview that is aligned with modern science. Modern physics, chemistry or biology have nothing to say about spirits. Modern technology operates without them. Weimar-era scholars, historians and philosophers, who promoted spiritualist perspectives in the humanities were honestly and openly anti-modern in their outlook. (This is something that authors such as Giedion or Pevsner avoided to admit and address.) Max Dvořák, for instance, dismissed the idea that only physical causation should be postulated in the explanations of historical events as "the superstition of causation."[89] Another Viennese art historian, Hans Sedlmayr, repudiated this idea as "coarse materialism," while the German historian Ernst Troeltsch opposed it as "psychologistic-positivist historiography."[90] Insofar as the modern worldview is to be understood as a worldview in line with modern science, Modernism in architecture could only stand for a decidedly anti-modern and intellectually conservative agenda. At the same time, Giedion and Pevsner were right when they endorsed spiritualism as a necessary element in their advocacy of modernist architecture. Without mysticism, no Modernism.

MODERNISM AFTER WORLD WAR TWO

Modernist architecture did, however, become dominant, and dominant in absolute terms, in the years that followed World War Two. This may seem to justify the exceptional attention that architectural historians have lavished on the modernist works from the decades preceding the war. It may be therefore pointed out that although in their time they belonged to a marginal stream of contemporary architecture, such works anticipated future developments. The architects who advocated Modernism before the second world war could not have been wrong, the argument will state, because modernist architecture did eventually become dominant globally. This global success of modernist architecture should be taken to mean that modernist architects were right in some sense. This argument is certainly cogent. Admittedly, one may respond that the argument does not establish that the global expansion of modernist architecture was any more desirable than some more recent phenomena such as global warming or the coronavirus pandemic. Had Nazis won World War Two, this would not mean that the Third Reich was something good. Nevertheless, it is undeniable that predictions of Le Corbusier, Mies, Gropius, and their accomplices turned out to be true, regardless of what one thinks about this outcome.

The discussion in the preceding section suggests two possible perspectives on and explanations of the global domination of Modernism after 1945. One may believe, together with Giedion and Pevsner, that there existed a spirit of the era that ultimately ensured the domination of the modernist idiom. A mysterious spiritual substance, in that case, would have exercised a massive, intellectual and cultural impact on clients, investors, architects across the globe and enforced the preference for modernist architecture. Maybe there are people who actually believe in such spirits and for them such an explanation is going to be credible. The alternative (materialist) explanation, that rejects the spiritualist perspective, starts from the observations that all these clients, investors, developers, architects who endorsed Modernism after World War Two had one thing in common: they were exposed to the same kind of economic pressures. Modernist architecture was cheaper to build and also to design, in an era of massive building programs (re-building of Europe, building boom in the USA). The important point was not only that ornamented façades cost more to build—in an era when architects were overloaded with work it was reasonable to omit ornamentation from buildings. Architecture offices simply did not have, nor could they pay, the drafting force that would enable them to keep working the way they did in the early decades of the twentieth century. The rise of Modernism coincides with the moment when it became a commercial necessity.

If this is so, and if the domination of Modernism after World War Two was caused by the economic situation, then this makes the founding fathers of the modernist movement only partly responsible for the bad consequences of Modernism and its general unpopularity among the general public. Modernism did not become dominant because of what they preached. They did preach it, but their preaching would not have had significant effects without the world war and the massive (re-)building programs that followed it. Admittedly, modernists did argue from the beginning that their architecture was cheaper to build. Even before World War One they advertised their approach to design as developer-friendly. Very early in the history of the modernist movement Loos observed that a real-estate speculator would normally favor apartment buildings that are only covered with plaster and without ornaments.[91] However, he complained, people would not want to live in such buildings. The hurdle became irrelevant once modernists started addressing housing for the poorest strata of society. Cheap social housing was a persistent theme in CIAM conferences and the main topic of the second congress in Frankfurt in 1929. Le Corbusier there discussed the accommodation of families with four children in 45m^2 apartments.[92] Before that, in *Toward an Architecture* he used the French government's plan to build 500,000 low-budget workers' apartments in ten years in order to argue in favor of Modernism.[93] It would also be hard to argue that in the years after the second world war Miesian boxes became widespread because of their aesthetic appeal. Rather, they were cheaper to build per square foot than the competition.[94] From the perspective of the architectural profession the fact that they required less labor to design and draft would have been even more important. It was thus the universality of economic pressures in the years after World War Two that brought about the global domination of Modernist architecture. These pressures even made no difference between Capitalism and Communism. At a conference of builders and architects in 1954, the first secretary of the Soviet Communist Party, Nikita Khrushchev, criticized architects who excessively decorate buildings and thus waste state funds.[95] It is hard to think that officials of western governments or powerful CEOs were less philistine. In the era of the Cold War, the common enemy of both western and communist leaders were the architects who would ornament the buildings they designed. Once the social-economic context in which Modernism became dominant is considered, it becomes hard to blame the pre-world-war modernist movement for the kind of architecture that came to dominate urban environments. Had there been no modernist movement in the decades before the second world war, the same cheap architecture that lacks aesthetic appeal would have resulted from the urgent and massive building programs of the late 1940s and the 1950s anyway. It is nevertheless true that the advocates of Modernism provided the theoretical justification for it. Their views became the ideology of the commercialization and the de-aestheticization of the profession after 1945. Without the world war and its economic consequences, the impact of the generation of modernist architects born in the 1880s (such as Le Corbusier, Mies and Gropius) would have been comparable of that of modernists whose zenith was in the years before the first world war, such as Peter Behrens, Hendrik Petrus Berlage, Otto Wagner or Adolf Loos. Without World War Two the dominant architectural idiom in the 1940s and the 1950s would still have been based on historical precedents, classical or neo-Gothic. Modernist architects would have been remembered as interesting individuals with some radical ideas but little impact on general architectural production. Some doctoral student, one can imagine, would have written an interesting dissertation about a bizarre group of architects-mystics who believed in spiritual substances that determine the course of history and who inferred from that belief that they should design buildings with unornamented facades and flat roofs—but that would have been all.

SKELETON IN THE CLOSET

During the decades that followed World War Two the suppression of classicist approaches to architecture became complete. This also pertains to architectural education, where the long-term consequences of this suppression have been particularly severe and they are strongly felt even today. Both before and after World War Two Classicism was a target of persistent attacks by the advocates of Modernism—

by far more than, for instance, the neo-Gothic tradition. In general, modernist architects and theorists were inclined to relativism, and this colored their attitude towards a tradition that they associated with timeless values. Temporal relativism that they preached was a general worldview and not limited to architectural matters. Gropius thus claimed:

> *Science has discovered the relativity of all human values and that they are in constant flux. There is no such thing as finality or eternal truth according to science.*[96]

One can hardly resist to ask whether it is eternally true that there are no eternal truths. As for science, the claim is plainly false. There are many scientifically established facts. For instance, it is an astronomical fact that Earth goes around the Sun and not vice-versa. Nevertheless, corybantic self-contradictions of this kind permeate the writings of modernists and their followers from Mendelsohn (who talked about the relativity of facts) and Giedion (who asserted the impossibility of objective judgments) to Peter Eisenman (who claimed that truth changes with the course of history) and Patrik Schumacher (who claimed that the epoch of universal truths is over).[97] None of them has ever explained whether it is an absolute fact that all facts are relative, whether it is an objective judgment that objective judgments are impossible, whether the variability of truth through history may itself be variable or whether it is a universal truth that the epoch of universal truths is over.* Logically lame relativism is far from being the worst argument against the classical tradition that one can find in modernist literature. Bruno Zevi, for instance, claimed that symmetry in buildings equals homosexuality.[98] At the time he made this claim this was meant to be a condemnation. The claim is as convincing as the suggestion that people who dislike symmetrical architecture are homophobes. Various authors from Mies van der

---

* If it is not an absolute fact that some facts are relative, then some facts can be absolute and not relative. If it is only a subjective judgment that no judgments are objective, then it is merely a personal view that does not preclude the possibility of objective judgments. If all truth changes through history, then this changeability ought to be changeable as well. In that case, at some point in time, some truths would not change through history. If it is not a universal truth that the epoch of universal truths is over, then when considering some aspects of the epoch (for instance in some parts of the world) universal truths may be possible.

Rohe to Peter Eisenman have complained that clients who commission classical buildings are motivated by nostalgia or the need to legitimate themselves.[99] This is possibly sometimes true, but it is also true that some clients who commission designs from cutting-edge "avant-garde" architects do so in order to present themselves as intellectuals. There is no reason to think that fake intellectualism that motivates some clients to commission buildings from "avant-garde" architects is less kitsch than nostalgic sentimentalism. Another bizarre argument that was often repeated in the early decades of the twentieth century is that people who live in classically designed buildings should be wearing togas or similar clothes from the past.[100] Following similar reasoning, an engineer who uses Pythagoras's Theorem in his or her calculations should dress as an ancient Greek. A particularly malicious form of defamation was the tendency to associate classical architecture with totalitarian regimes, mainly by pointing to Albert Speer's participation in the Nazi government. In fact, modernist architects often sought chances to collaborate with totalitarian governments and expressed their endorsement for totalitarian ideologies. Frank Lloyd Wright travelled to the USSR in 1937, during the worst purge in Soviet history and expressed praise for the Soviet regime.[101] The claim that Mies and Gropius left Germany because of political persecution has been thoroughly debunked by more recent scholarship.[102] They certainly did not hesitate to engage or participate in the propagandist endeavors of the Third Reich.[103] Former Bauhaus students massively contributed to the military efforts of the Third Reich.[104] Le Corbusier similarly sought patronage both from Soviet dictatorship and the Vichy puppet government.[105] Modernist architects assembled in CIAM made huge efforts to organize their fourth congress in Moscow under Stalin. It is true that modernists were less successful than classicists when competing for commissions for monumental buildings, both in totalitarian and democratic political systems. This can hardly be surprising, considering that in the 1930s none of them could show more than a meager portfolio of monumental work. In fact, the very idea that a monumental modernist building is possible was controversial during the era.[106] Only a debate initiated by Giedion in the 1940s would theorize the possibility of monumental modernist buildings.[107]

The argument about clothes from the past eras mentioned above is particularly interesting because of the relativist assumptions that it reveals and takes for granted. The supposition is that values of architecture (aesthetic or otherwise) are relative to time the way this is the case with clothing fashions. In other words, that architecture cannot have trans-cultural and trans-temporal values. It is, however, far from obvious that aesthetic values change so easily. It is not obvious that they do not have transcultural stability comparable, for instance, to Pythagoras's theorem. It is undeniable that people today do relate aesthetically to older buildings and buildings in historical styles. Repeatedly, the destruction of such buildings has led to mass protests. (It does not help to dismiss these protests as motivated by nostalgia. The response will be that modernist architecture indeed makes people nostalgic for old building styles. If people trusted modernist architects to make something nicer, they would not protest.) We do not loose the capacity to appreciate buildings from the past as the time goes. Very often, the same architectural works have been consistently appreciated for their aesthetic values for centuries.

At the same time, it is not hard to think of credible alternatives to relativism. One may, for instance, argue that the appeal of some types of ornaments (such as the classical orders) derives from the fact that they were developed and gradually improved by generations of architects. Over centuries, various architects introduced changes and sought to make improvements. Those changes that were deemed successful were adopted and further perfected by other architects. As Palladio put it, beautiful inventions made by one generation of architects enable further investigation of new ideas.[108] Historically, one can indeed document gradual refinement of forms of various elements of the classical orders, such as Doric capitals or Ionic volutes. The fact that many highly competent architects worked on perfecting the system of the classical orders can be taken to explain its wide appeal even today. (This view is not unlike Geoffrey Scott's characterization of Renaissance architecture as the "experimental science of taste."[109]) The background assumption is that preferences for some spatial forms and their combinations are generally shared by most humans. The fact that modern people often attribute aesthetic properties to the same works that were also appreciated in the past can be invoked to support this assumption. An additional argument are compositional similarities between architectural works that have no common historical source— for instance, the use of the same principles of monumental composition in Mediterranean and Pre-Columbian architecture. If one surveys the history of architecture globally, one will find that symmetry reigns supreme in architectural works of civilizations that were never in contact with each other. Except for our modern era when it has been consciously suppressed, it is hard to find periods or civilizations in which symmetry did not dominate architectural production. Unless one is willing to rely on spiritual substances in the explanation of such trans-cultural phenomena, one has to think that they result from the nature of the human mind and the way it is structured to prefer some particular spatial arrangements. Readers with materialist inclinations, who believe that human mental processes result from the neurology of the brain, may further assume that some formal-aesthetic preferences are hard-wired. This would be the view that human brain derives pleasure from some combinations of shapes and colors independently of ideas that one associates with them. Arguably, this would bring us back to Scott's formalist views with which our discussion started. At this moment neurobiology and cognitive science cannot prove or disprove the possibility that the capacity for purely formal enjoyments is hard-wired to the human brain. This also means that the proponents of aesthetic relativism cannot preclude such a possibility. In any case, the hypothesis is certainly more credible than the belief in spiritual substances that decide about the appropriateness of specific stylistic preferences to certain eras.

It is, in fact, nothing short of paradoxical that the advocates of Modernism employed ideas from the distinctly anti-modern German philosophy of history. This certainly indicates their poor understanding of the ideas they relied on. As mentioned, the philosophers and historians who postulated spiritual forces in history were anti-materialists and opposed to the worldview of modern science. Their important thesis was that immaterial, spiritual forces do play a role in history. They precisely argued that such forces have genuine causal capacities that modern science cannot explain. Insofar as it is accepted that modern worldview has to be compatible with that of modern science, it necessarily precludes the belief in such forces. They cannot be invoked in order to justify claims about the appropriateness of certain architectural shapes to the modern era. Aesthetic formalism and approaches to design motivated by visual-formal aesthetic concerns were immediate victims of the spiritualism-based requirement that architecture should express its time. Obviously, it can be responded that the urgency of housing problems in the decades after World War Two justified the suppression of aesthetic issues. Mass building projects built in those years did provide better living and working conditions for millions of people. This is true, but one should also not forget that cheaply designed architecture is rarely better architecture. Looking long term, one should bear in mind that architects do not merely develop the skills to do the kind of architecture that they commonly do. They also *lose* the skills that they do not use. Young architects fail to acquire the skills that they are not taught. The quarter of century spent on designing mass housing and cheap public buildings unavoidably changed the architectural profession beyond recognition. By the 1970s, when architects woke up from the dream about a better world built cheaply and designed with little drafting effort and without concern for aesthetic matters, the reality became a nightmare.

PHENOMENOLOGY

Gregor Samsa, the main character in a story by Franz Kafka, woke up one morning transformed into a giant cockroach.[110] Kafka describes the gradual process by which Gregor became aware of his new physical form, the painful realization that his family members react to him with disgust, his inability to use language in order to communicate with them, their embarrassment and efforts to contain him in his room, and eventually their relief and happiness when they realize that he has died. The story can be read as a disturbing metaphor for the reception of modernist architecture by the general public some decades after the second world war—when it became obvious that the dream of making a better world produced an ugly glass-and-concrete desert. The way it happens in Kafka's story, it took time before the general public became aware of the consequences of Modernism. The original surprise was replaced by disbelief, that was further replaced by efforts to understand the novelty and be sympathetic. After communication with the architectural profession turned out to be impossible, the general public initiated efforts to contain the vermin and protect historical urban environments from destruction and modernist intrusion.

This is, however, where the metaphor stops. In Kafka's story the giant cockroach, that was once Gregor Samsa, eventually died. It would be naïve to think that this happened with Modernism in architecture. Charles Jencks even optimistically identified its death with the demolition of Pruitt-Igoe residential complex in St Louis, Missouri in 1972. However, it seems more accurate to say (paraphrasing Garrison Keillor) that things merely got worse before they got worse. Kafka's Gregor Samsa was a benign character, sympathetic to the plight of his family. He was genuinely trying to be helpful, even though he did not know how. But Kafka never considered the darker sides of the human soul, pride, obstinacy and denial. Perceptive architects certainly realized where things were going much before the 1970s. As early as the mid-1950s Gropius admitted that his generation was guilty for "producing horrors of repetitive housing developments."[111]

A decade later Mies expressed no regrets: "The sociologists tell us we have to think about the human beings who are living in that building. That is a sociological problem, not an architectural one."[112] For the past half a century the reaction of the architectural profession has generally followed Mies's attitude. The rise of the Obfuscatory Turn in architectural theory started in the 1970s and it cannot be accidental that it coincided with the moment when the failure of Modernism became a publicly recognized fact. By the late 1980s the dominant response of the architecture profession and academics was that nothing unpleasant has happened. The view of the architects and theorists who endorsed Deconstruction was that architecture was never meant to make human lives or the human environment better. More precisely, their post-humanist position was that humans do not exist, that they are social constructs. This response to the crisis created by Modernism will be analyzed in the next chapter. Another response that one can trace since the early 1970s has been associated with the phenomenological tradition in philosophy. It seeks to overcome the unpleasant consequences of Modernism by rejecting the rational, science-based worldview that (these authors believe) actually generated the crisis. This perspective is the subject of the current chapter.

CHRISTIAN NORBERG-SCHULZ

"Phenomenology" is a long word, and people who use such words look learned. The term has its definite meaning in philosophy; in architecture its meaning is much more vague. It was the Norwegian architectural theorist Christian Norberg-Schulz who drew attention to phenomenology and Martin Heidegger's work during the 1970s. The lasting contribution of Norberg-Schulz's phenomenological approach to architecture was his introduction of obfuscation as a methodological tool in architectural theory. In many ways he is the founding father of the Obfuscatory Turn in architecture. This method came to dominate theoretical writings on architecture during the final decades of the twentieth century. Already in 1963, before his endorsement of Heidegger, in the book *Intentions in Architecture*, Norberg-Schulz formulated important elements of (what was to become) the phenomenological approach to architecture. The book introduced into architectural theory the idea that our perception of objects is inseparable from the recognition of these objects, that all seeing is seeing-as.[113] On this account, human perception always depends on what we know and believe about the things we see and on how we classify them. "The given world consists of things we know," he says, and "we perceive the sum of our experiences and these experiences are in the highest degree a result of the demands made by the society."[114]

This view was widely influential at the time he was writing, due to the impact of *Gestalt* and so-called "New Look" psychology of the 1950s.[115] By introducing this perspective into architectural theory, Norberg-Schulz made a contribution to the discipline equivalent to the one Ernst Gombrich made to art history with his book *Art and Illusion*, Thomas Kuhn to the history of science with his *Structure of Scientific Revolutions*, Nelson Goodman to aesthetics with his *Languages of Art* and Arthur Danto to the philosophy of history with his *Analytical Philosophy of History*.[116] Together with *Intentions in Architecture*, all these books came out in the 1960s. They all introduced into their respective disciplines the idea that perception is inseparable from the classification of the perceived objects. In other words, they insisted that things cannot be perceived independently of how they are conceptualized—that seeing always depends on beliefs and expectations one has about things seen. This was also the dominant view in the psychology of perception of the era. It should be mentioned that this understanding of human perception is regarded as antiquated by psychologists today. The standard view of modern psychology is that the functioning of the parts of the brain that form our visual experience is impenetrable for classifications, conceptual thinking, beliefs, expectations or associations.[117]

In the second half of the twentieth century, when it was on the height of its influence, the view that all perception depends on one's conceptual thinking and beliefs was often combined with another claim: that conceptual frameworks and beliefs of individuals result from their social, cultural or linguistic contexts. As for architectural theory, the most obvious consequence of the view that all perception is inseparable from classification was that it made the position that Scott described as "romantic fallacy" unavoidable. If one cannot even perceive architectural works independently of the ideas one associates with them, then one certainly cannot attribute to them aesthetic qualities independently of these ideas. Phenomenological positions in architectural theory typically assume that architectural works cannot be valued on the basis of their formal, visual, spatial merits, but only on the basis of stories, narratives, meanings associated with them. In architectural education, this view resulted in the suppression of visual concerns. It produced generations of architects who were able to talk well about the buildings they designed but were also systematically trained to disregard the way their buildings looked. In architectural history, Norberg-Schulz's claim that one does not perceive shapes, but "meaningful forms" led to the suppression of interest in spatial, visual and formal aspects of architectural works.[118] It implied that architectural historians should study "meanings," narratives that were associated with them. In his own writings, the approach led to the fabrication of historical claims that had no grounding in credible scholarship. Norberg-Schulz's discussions of "meanings" of architectural works regularly relied on his own associations (more accurately, prejudices) that he projected on various historical contexts without being able to document his claims. He thus claimed that the Gothic Cathedral was heaven for medieval man, that in the stone age menhirs were understood as abodes of the vital power while dolmens were symbols of femininity, that Egyptian pyramids constitute an artificial row of mountains, that the disposition of buildings in the sanctuary in Delphi looks haphazard because "as representatives of Greek democratic society, none of them were allowed to dominate the others," that columns in the temple of Apollo in Corinth lack entasis (the curved swelling of the shaft) because they express the abstract, intellectual strength of the god.[119] Obviously, there are no documents that could confirm any of these claims. Norberg-Schulz mainly relied on his own fantasies in order be able to state "meanings" that people of the past associated with architectural works. He also claimed that these "meanings" pre-exist social contexts and that they are merely discovered by architects.[120]

Idealism (also referred to as *anti-realism*) is a particularly important consequence of the view that the way people perceive things *always* depends on how they classify these things and what they believe about them. Starting from Norberg-Schulz's early writings, Idealism came to dominate architectural theory for decades. Imagine that I perceive two things, one red and another blue. Imagine also that I classify them according to their colors. Consider now the question of, why I classify them so. If all seeing is inseparable from classification, then it cannot be the case that I first perceived their colors, established that one of them is red and another blue and then classified them as red and blue. The thesis that "all seeing is seeing as" precisely claims that *I could not have* perceived their color independently of how I classified (conceptualized) them. I had to classify them *first*, decide that they belong under the concept "red" or "blue," in order to see them as red or blue. It follows that the way things are perceived is independent of the way things physically are. The way we see things—the color we perceive, in this example—then depends exclusively on how we classify them *before* we see them, what we believe about them. It does not depend, for instance, on the color of the light they reflect. For many people, this conclusion borders on absurdity. It can be seen as a refutation of the view that all seeing depends on classification. Norberg-Schulz, however, explicitly endorsed such anti-realism: "We do not simply perceive a world which is common to all of us, as naïve realists maintain, but different worlds which are a product of our motivations and past experiences."[121] This view was very widespread at the time when he was writing. A well-known example from the same era is Thomas Kuhn's claim that after the change of the scientific paradigm scientists "live in a different world."[122] Idealism (anti-realism) has massive implications for the understanding of the built environment. When Norberg-Schulz says that the Gothic cathedral *was* heaven for contemporary man, this is a claim about the world in which medieval men lived and not merely a metaphorical statement about their beliefs.[123] The assumption is not that we live in the same world, whereby different peoples or cultures interpret it differently. Rather, it is supposed that people from different centuries or cultures actually live in different worlds in which, for instance, even physical laws can differ. From the beginning, authors who have endorsed phenomenological approaches to architecture have tended towards the idealist view that the physical reality is constructed by the social, cultural or linguistic forces. Dalibor Vesely, another architectural theorist belonging to the phenomenological school, for instance, claimed that reality is not something fixed and absolute, but "always a result of our ability to experience, visualize, and articulate."[124] Alberto Pérez-Gómez—arguably the most prominent architectural historian among advocates of phenomenological approaches to architecture— asserted that "the objective world does not exist," that it is an illusion, and that the reality of the modern world "is not independent of our consciousness."[125] It is important to understand the implications of such an anti-realist position. Consider, for instance, Perez-Gomez's claim that "The verb 'to see' was reciprocal in Greek; whoever saw was seen, and the blind were invisible."[126] This view assumes that

49

if the grammatical form of the verb "to see" in some language does not differentiate between the active and passive forms, then *in the reality* of these people "whoever saw was seen, and the blind were invisible." In other words, reality is merely a linguistic construct and it depends on the grammar of the language that people use to talk about it. The grammar of the language that people speak, from this point of view, decides the physical properties of the reality that they live in. (It should be also mentioned that as regards Greek grammar, the claim that "to see" was "reciprocal" is actually false.[127])

The next chapter will analyze some more extreme ramifications of Idealism. At this moment it is useful to clarify the terminology used in the discussion. The use of the term "Idealism" is appropriate insofar as we are discussing a position that denies that the material world exists on its own or claims that it is constructed by immaterial forces or human consciousness. "Idealism" is the opposite of "materialism." For instance, the use of the term "idealist" is suitable for an author who assumes that cultures, languages or social forces exist independently of the material world and create that world. This would be the view that, for instance, languages or cultures do not result from interactions between biological human individuals but pre-exist human society and construct the material world that makes biological humans possible. The use of the term "romantic" in this book is in line with Scott's definition of the "romantic fallacy" discussed in the previous chapter—i.e. the assumption that architecture is not to be evaluated on the basis of its formal properties but on the basis of ideas associated with it. "Romantic Idealism" that came to dominate architectural theory during the Obfuscatory Turn beginning with the 1970s is a combination of these two positions.

HEIDEGGERIZATION OF ARCHITECTURAL THEORY

It is in the context of these wider views on architecture and the physical reality that we have to understand Norberg-Schulz's interest in Heidegger's philosophy. At the same time as he endorsed idealist anti-realism and adopted heideggerian methods of asserting theoretical claims, he also pioneered the use of obfuscation as a method of arguing in architectural theory. It may seem obvious that there must be a link between the two. Heidegger's own writings are notorious for obfuscation and the lack of clarity. Famously, his pretentious and unclear use of language have been mocked and regarded as comical by numerous prominent intellectuals including Thomas Mann, Günter Grass and Gabriel Marcel.[128] The proliferation of obscure texts on architecture after the 1970s may be seen as a result of Heidegger's influence, an epidemic with Norberg-Schulz as the patient zero. It is, however, important to bear in mind the wider picture.

Obfuscation as a rhetorical tool in philosophy has been known at least since the times of sophists in ancient Greece. The tendency to regard those who employ it as charlatans is probably as old. More than two centuries ago, Immanuel Kant wrote:

> It is utterly ridiculous when someone speaks and decides like a genius in matters of that require careful rational investigation. When this happens, one does not know whether one should laugh about the charlatan that spreads so much mist around himself, whereby the less one can infer clearly the more one is allowed to dissimulate—or should one laugh about the public that naively believes that his incapacity to achieve clarity results from droves of new truths that come to him.[129]

Admittedly, most philosophers active in philosophy departments in English-speaking countries today would easily agree that Heidegger is precisely a thinker of the kind that Kant described. Analytic philosophers, who traditionally dominate English-speaking philosophy departments, typically take a very dim view of Heidegger's philosophy. In their view, it is the clear formulation of arguments that differentiates philosophy of from incomprehensible poetry. Graham Harman has recently expressed the view that Heidegger's reputation among analytic philosophers has improved over time and shifted from "unintelligible poet and pompous mystic" to something like "non-mentalist verificationist anti-realist."[130] However, it is hard to imagine an analytic philosopher who could stomach Heidegger's paragraphs such as:

> In the midst of total Being there presences an open place. There is a clearing. Considered from the position of Being, it is beinger than Being. This open middle is therefore not surrounded by Being, but the cleared middle surrounds all Being as nothing, that we hardly know.[131]

Insofar as truth happens as the original conflict between clearing and hiding, earth rises only through the world, while the world is founded only on earth. But how does truth happen? We respond: it happens in few essential ways. One of these ways in which truth happens, is the work-being of work. The erecting of the world and the producing of earth is the work that the disputation of the dispute, in which the unhiddenness of Being in totality, truth, is fought for.[132]

This widespread criticism of Heidegger makes it necessary to emphasize that our topic here is not Heidegger's own use of obfuscation in his philosophy. It is conceivable that some readers of this book may endorse the harshest criticism of Heidegger's work. They may see in it philosophical charlatanry that is as intellectually barren (and even comical) as Heidegger's own political views were evil. (He was a Nazi.) This *philosophical* evaluation of Heidegger's work cannot be our topic here. The judgment may be legitimate, but it should be left for books about *his* philosophy. Our topic here is the use of obfuscation by architects and architectural theorists, not by Heidegger himself. Similarly, both paragraphs cited above belong to the essay "The Origin of the Work of Art," one of two texts by Heidegger that are very often cited by architects and theorists who advocate phenomenological approaches to architecture. Insofar as one thinks that such paragraphs are meaningless—which seems hard to deny—one is certainly tempted to regard the authors who pretend to understand them as impostors. This line of reasoning is maybe justified, but it is also not particularly interesting for our discussion here. Rather, our topic here is the use of obfuscation that has accompanied heideggerian influences in architectural theory since the 1970s.

Consider, as an example, Norberg-Schulz's discussion of Heidegger's essays "Building, Dwelling, Thinking" and "The Origin of the Work of Art." A bridge, says Heidegger in "Building, Dwelling, Thinking," "collects earth around it as a landscape. It does not just connect banks that are already there. The banks emerge as banks only as the bridge crosses the stream."[133] Norberg-Schulz infers from this that the bridge creates the place.[134] The words "earth" and "landscape", he says, are not topographical concepts; rather, they designate a "thing" that appears through the "collecting" that is performed by the bridge.[135] In the other essay, "The Origin of the Work of Art," Heidegger claims that a Greek temple and its precinct collect around itself the unity of paths and relations in which birth and death, doom and blessing, victory and disgrace, endurance and decay win for mankind the form of its destiny.[136] Norberg-Schulz explains that a temple was chosen by Heidegger as an example of a work that brings to light something that is hidden.[137] Heidegger calls this something "truth", he explains, and a building can be an artwork and it "preserves" truth. In Heidegger's description the temple makes visible all things of the earth and heaven: cliffs, sea, air and so on. In general, says Norberg-Schulz, "it opens a world and places it back on the earth" and thus "puts truth into effect."[138] He makes the general claim that "...works of architecture ... *embody* existential meanings, making the world stand forth as it is."[139]

The reason why grandiloquent claims like these sound profound is that they are plainly false or meaningless. Architectural works *do not* and *cannot* make the world stand. Norberg-Schulz's claims are certainly false if we take the term "stand" literally, and it is unclear what they mean if we take the term metaphorically. It is plainly false that a temple makes cliffs, sea or air visible. Cliffs or sea would be visible even if no temples existed; air is invisible in any case. Also, it is utterly meaningless to say that a temple "opens a world and places it back on the earth" or that it "puts truth into effect." The claim that buildings "preserve" truth depends on defining "truth" as something that a temple brings to light. We are never told what this might be. (Many buildings "preserve" mice and cockroaches, but one would hardly identify them with "truth.")

Another good example of the use of obfuscation in order to generate the impression of profundity is Norberg-Schulz analysis of Heidegger's "fourfold"—earth, sky, mortals and divinities—from the essay "Building, Dwelling, Thinking." This "fourfold" is a notoriously unclear part of Heidegger's philosophy. Graham Harman, who is generally sympathetic to Heidegger, admits that "[n]one of Heidegger's basic concepts has been more ridiculed than the fourfold."[140] Karstens Harries, also sympathetic to Heidegger, opens his explanation of the fourfold with a rather unpromising citation:

In the simplicity of its own united fourfold, the thing thingly stays the united four; Earth, Sky, Divinities and Mortals.[141]

In fact, Heidegger's own pronouncements about the nature of the elements of the fourfold—as mentioned, Earth, Sky, Divinities and Mortals—typically do not sound particularly complex. (The occasional use of a series of simple and obvious statements that border on banality was one of his favorite rhetorical strategies.) About mortals, for instance, he says that "Mortals are humans. They are called mortals because they can die. To die means to be able to death as death..."[142] He provides similar, rather straightforward, explanations for the remaining three elements of the fourfold. It is, rather, the philosophical claims about the fourfold that make experts in his philosophy and commentators uncomfortable. Remarkably, these claims also made Heidegger's "fourfold" a favorite theme of phenomenologically oriented architectural theorists. We shall see some entertaining examples of such endorsements later in this chapter. Norberg-Schulz explains that the elements of the fourfold "reflect others. They all belong in the 'mirror game' that constitutes the world."[143] Heidegger, Norberg-Schulz says, defined "the world which is gathered by the thing as a 'fourfold,'" since the original meaning of "thing" is "gathering."[144] He thus concludes that "the things are what they are relative to the basic structure of the world. The things make the world appear, and therefore condition the man."[145] Applied to dwelling, he infers, this means that "dwelling primarily consists in the appropriation of a world of things, not in a material sense, but as an ability to interpret the meaning the things gather."[146] One may, however, respond that things are large sets of molecules. Some people attribute meanings to some things, but no thing can gather meanings by itself. We are never told what is wrong with this alternative view about the basic structure of the world that is in line with the worldview of modern science.

By this time, the functioning of obfuscation as an argumentational method should be obvious. When he invokes Heidegger, Norberg-Schulz includes series of counterintuitive claims that cannot be challenged. Every counterargument is blocked by the possible claims that words are used with a different, more profound meaning. When he states that the banks of the river come about only when the bridge is built, it is pointless to argue that a bridge cannot be built if no banks exist. The response will be that the word "banks" is used with a different, more profound, meaning. These meanings, however, are never stated. It is pointless to argue that one can live in a house without interpreting meanings, because we will be told that to dwell in a house is something more than to live in a house. We will never be told what the difference is. It is similarly pointless to argue that buildings do not preserve truth, because the response will be that the words "language," "building," or "truth" are used with some non-standard, more profound meaning. These profound meanings are never explained.

Counterintuitive claims proliferate and they can never be challenged, because we cannot know what these claims mean. Rather, we are supposed to believe that they state something profound. The reason for this is that Norberg-Schulz is summarizing Heidegger's statements, and Heidegger was a profound thinker. A grumpy analytic philosopher may observe here that Heidegger is known to be a profound thinker because he made profound statements, whereby these statements are known to be profound because they were made by a profound thinker. One may agree or disagree with this criticism. However, once we are told that words do not mean what they normally mean, and Norberg-Schulz does not explain what he means when he uses them, it becomes impossible to understand what he is saying. And we certainly have the right to doubt that he had any idea either. As Friedrich Nietzsche put it once, "those who know that they are profound strive for clarity, while those who would like to seem profound to the crowd strive for obscurity."[147]

TOWARDS A GENERAL THEORY OF OBFUSCATION: ELEMENTS OF A TYPOLOGY

The rise of the Obfuscatory Turn in architectural discussions during the final decades of the twentieth century is a remarkable phenomenon of the architectural history of the era. Starting from the 1970s, obfuscation became a core tool in the advocacy of theoretical and design positions, in a sharp contrast to the situation in the previous decades. Nothing similar, for instance, can be traced in the writings of modernist architects and theorists of earlier in the century. Towards the end of this book we shall investigate the motivation behind the Obfuscatory Turn and why it happened exactly during this era. As for now, it is important to examine the forms of obfuscation that were employed. Since it was the authors belonging to the phenomenological tradition who initiated the trend, it is relevant to start by presenting a typology of their contributions to the phenomenon. We shall see later that subsequent contributors radicalized the forms of obfuscation but did not step out of the phenomenologists' groundbreaking work. They did not invent new types of obfuscation that are not already described here.

In principle, one should differentiate between obfuscatory strategies that rely on singular obfuscatory statements and those that achieve cumulative obfuscation by combining multiple statements.

In the first category belong types of obfuscation such as *obfuscation plain and simple, profound banality, pretentious falsity* and the *jargon of profundity*. Two most significant models of cumulative obfuscation are *salads* and *cumulative banalities*. The way these strategies work is best understood if we consider examples.

In the case of *obfuscation plain and simple* the author generates incomprehensible sentences by using terms that readers are supposed to recognize as Heideggerian and thus indicative of profound thoughts. (It's a little bit like replacing the speedometer in your car with one that can measure much higher speeds in order to convince people that your car is much faster than it really is.) The sentences used for the purpose typically have no detectable meaning. Often, however, they do indicate that the author knows unusual words and philosophical terms. The reader then can infer that the author is reporting some profound insights. Occasionally, a direct mentioning of Heidegger himself in such contexts can be used to reassure the reader that the author is capable of deep thoughts because he or she reads and understands such a profound thinker as Heidegger. Consider, as an example, the following statement by Juhani Pallasmaa:

> *Every art needs to be reconnected with its ontological essence, particularly at periods when the art form tends to turn into an empty aestheticised mannerism.*[148]

The fatuousness of the statement becomes obvious the moment we ask what these "ontological" essences might be. When is an essence ontological and when is it not? Do arts have both ontological and non-ontological essences and how can we differentiate between them? What does it mean to "reconnect" art with its essence? Normally, essence is that what something is, so how can something be *disconnected* from its essence, which is that what it is? (Can we use an electric cable to reconnect them?) Another example is Norberg-Schulz's explanation of Heidegger's statement that humans dwell "between work and word":

> *Word opens the world, while work gives it presence. In the work the world is placed back to the earth, that is, it becomes part of immediate here and now, whereby the last-mentioned appears in its existence.*[149]

It is impossible to say what this statement might mean, but it certainly suggests its author's deep thoughts.

Profound banality is a form of obfuscation in which a fairly simple and banal thought is dressed in a terminology that makes it appear profound. A good example is Kenneth Frampton's use of the term "ontological" in order to refer to the physical, bearing structure of a building.[150] Similarly, Frampton describes as a "change ... of an epistemic nature" the fact Mies van der Rohe in his projects after 1944 made the connection between columns and beams became visible.[151] "Epistemic" is something that pertains to cognition, and when the connection between columns and beams becomes obvious, it is presumably "epistemic." (Following the same reasoning, the cereal I've had for breakfast this morning was epistemic because I could see it.)

Situations when an author describes an ordinary architectural situation using words that suggests philosophical profundity are also versions of a profound banality. Norberg-Schulz captions the picture of the columns that stand on the stony platform of the Hephaisteion temple in Athens with the words "[t]he setting-into-work of standing."[152] The sophisticated reader is meant to recognize that he is referring to Heidegger's view that art is "setting-into-work-of-the-truth-of-being."[153] Frampton similarly describes the earthwork of Louis Kahn's Kimbell Art Museum as a factor in "the manifest integration of the building into its site" that "evoke[s] the presence of nature in a more telluric aspect."[154] (The Latin word "tellus" means "earth," and "telluric" is therefore by definition something that pertains to the soil. Every earthwork is "telluric." If I have to walk through mud, I can also say that I am experiencing nature "in a more telluric aspect.") Kahn was thus able, according to Frampton, "to inscribe the Kimbell into its site in such a way as to establish a categoric 'clearing' and to endow the resultant precinct with a particular presence."[155] (The use of the word "clearing" makes the statement profound because it relates it to Heidegger's paragraph about "clearing" cited earlier in this chapter. In the case of Kahn's building, this means that trees, houses, dumpsters and similar that were originally on the site had to be removed for the building to be built.) Frampton further infers that Kahn's project demonstrates the importance that Heidegger attached to boundary, by saying "[a] boundary (*peras*) is not something at which something stops but ... that from which something begins its presencing."[156] (Norberg-Schulz also likes citing this insight of Heidegger's.[157]) Heidegger (and ancient Greek words such as *peras*) provide us thus with the profound insight that if a building is surrounded by earthwork, then it has to be on one side of the earthwork. The insight that when something ends at a line, then something else has to be on the other side of the line may seem to be banal. However, it has to be profound, since it comes from Heidegger. One certainly has to be impressed by Heideggerian phrases such as "begins its presencing." (My cat likes spending time in the kitchen, waiting for me to open the fridge. My fridge therefore gathers the presencing of cathood and makes it firmly rooted in the kitchen.)

Another similar example by Frampton is his discussion of two sketches made by Jørn Utzon in relation to his project of the church in Bagsvaerd (Denmark). In one of the drawings Utzon drew some people scattered on a walkway with some sky and clouds above. Frampton immediately jumps to infer that in the drawing "we seem to encounter an unconscious reference to the Heideggerian *Geviert* or 'foursome' ['fourfold']; to the Earth, the Sky, Divinities and Mortals."[158] Obviously, the same could be said of any drawing or painting of a group of humans under the sky. If the drawing or painting was made before Heidegger wrote his essay "Building, Dwelling, Thinking" one could even say that the author anticipated Heidegger's "fourfold." Since Heidegger's "fourfold" consists of earth and skies, mortals and divinities, one can always provide a profound "heideggerian interpretation" for any architectural work by pointing out that it is between earth and sky. Presumably, this proves the universal applicability of Heidegger's thinking to architecture. A good example is Norberg-Schulz's statements that "[a] column ... keeps earth and sky apart and relates them to each other. ...[an] architrave belongs primarily to the earth, whereas a pediment relates earth and sky and thus possesses figural quality."[159]

Pretentious falsity is a form of obfuscation that consists in making obviously false statements that pretend to say something profound. Such statements dissimulate to convey some deeper insight and often look like metaphors. However, the profound meaning is actually missing. A good example is Heidegger's statement from "Building, Dwelling, Thinking": "When I go towards the exit of a room I am already there and would not be able to go there unless I was already there."[160] The obvious response is that if one goes somewhere it means that he or she is not there, and if he or she were there one could not go to that place. Although it is false, Heidegger's statement presumably sounds profound to some people. When Norberg-Schulz cites it, we have to take it as a clear indication of his ability to engage in such profound thoughts.[161] Pallasmaa's assertions about the role of smell and taste in human interactions with buildings belong to the same category. His claims that

> *Every touching experience is multi-sensory; qualities of matter, space, and scale are measured equally by the eye, ear, nose, skin, tongue, skeleton and muscle. Architecture involves seven realms of sensory experience which interact and infuse each other.* [162]

Or:

> *The strongest memory of a space is often its odor.* [163]

These claims are simply false. The experience of touching objects is not multi-sensory. It is also not true that "qualities of matter, space, and scale are measured equally by the eye, ear, nose, skin, tongue, skeleton and muscle." A blind person cannot *see* things by *touching* them. Also, people cannot determine "qualities of space" such as the size or scale of buildings by *licking* buildings. One cannot *hear* the distance between a door and a window. An architect cannot establish the scale of a drawing on the basis of its *smell*. As for the claim about memory, it is impossible to remember odors so well as visual or auditory experiences. Visual and auditory experiences can be *recalled* in imagination. For instance, one can imagine seeing a room or hearing a melody that one heard earlier. However, one cannot *imagine* smells, tastes or tactile experiences from the past. One can only *recognize* them. Since such experiences cannot be recalled in imagination, they are often less relevant than visual and auditory experiences. A similar example is Norberg-Schulz's claim:

> *"... architectural forms ... are conditioned by a preordained place in which nature participates. Therefore, architecture is not a result of the actions of man, but rather it renders the world that makes these actions possible."* [164]

Presumably this is meant to be a deep thought, but it is plainly false: architecture cannot come into existence if nobody designs it nor builds it. People have to pre-exist buildings they build.

Sometimes a pretentious falsity is constructed by falsely attributing to a philosopher views aligned with those of architectural phenomenologists. Consider the following claim about Aristotle, made by Frampton:

Place, as an Aristotelian phenomenon, arises at a symbolic level with the conscious signification of social meaning and at a concrete level with the establishment of an articulate realm on which man or men may come into being.[165]

It is true that in his *Physics* Aristotle discussed the concept of place. However, he defined the place of a thing as the closest limit of the surrounding body.[166] When Frampton says that "as an Aristotelian phenomenon" place "arises at a symbolic level with the conscious signification of social meaning" one has to doubt whether he bothered to read Aristotle at all. For Aristotle, place could not arise at "symbolic level with the conscious signification of social meaning," because in his view, the place of the body is the surfaces that surround the body, plain and simple. To make things worse, Frampton claims that an articulate realm gets established on which men come into being and from which the place arises. He does not explain how there can be an articulate realm without human agents that would make it articulate.

A more complex example of a pretentious falsity is Norberg-Schulz's recounting of the story "Last man home" by the Norwegian writer Terjei Vesaas.[167] The story is a romantic glorification of nature as experienced by a young lumberjack who works in the forest and one day he hears the voice "here you are at home." We get told that "the forest discloses itself. His own place is revealed." The young man stays long time in the forest after trees have spoken to him. As a literary work Vesaas's story may be an interesting description of the ways some people imagine that they relate to their environment. But beyond this, as a basis for a theoretical position about architecture, such fantasies will not get us far. To put it bluntly: if Vesaas describes a *real* situation, then the young lumberjack needs psychiatric help. If these voices that he hears induce him to stay excessive time in Norwegian forests, he may have unpleasant experiences, encounter dangerous animals or even die of hypothermia. Listening to what trees have to say cannot be a serious proposition for how humans should relate to forests. Similarly, as a thesis relevant for architectural theory, Norberg-Schulz's claim that buildings speak and that "those who have been open to listen, have beheld the 'saying' of works of architecture," can only be taken as a description of a condition that requires medical attention.[168] We cannot base our relationship to the built environment on hallucinations.

Jargon of profundity is arguably the most unkind form of obfuscation. It consists in a value-laden dismissal or approval in situations when the author has no arguments to present. Consider, once again, Pallasmaa's claim cited before:

> *Every art needs to be reconnected with its ontological essence, particularly at periods when the art form tends to turn into an empty aestheticised mannerism.*[169]

The use of the word "empty" is an example of the jargon of profundity. Together with words such as "superficial," "naïve" or "vulgar" (for instance, in phrases such as "superficial formalism," "naïve realism" or "vulgar materialism") such words are typically used in order to dismiss the views that an author does not like but cannot provide an argument against them. If an argument were available, the author would present it, instead of a value-laden but unsubstantiated dismissal. Something similar applies to words such as "profound" or "deep," insofar as they express unsubstantiated praise in situations when the author is unable to justify that praise. Consider another statement by Pallasmaa:

> *Profound architecture does not merely beautify the settings of dwelling: great buildings articulate the experiences of our very existence.*[170]

The terms "merely" and "profound" serve to devalue the efforts of all architects who sought to achieve beauty in their buildings, such as Leon Battista Alberti or Andrea Palladio. The value-laden dismissal is not substantiated, since it is not clear that efforts to "beautify the settings of dwellings" cannot produce great architecture. It is certainly legitimate to think, as Alberti put it, that beauty is "something great and divine, and in achieving it all powers of the arts and ingenuity are consumed."[171] It is also dubious that, as Pallasmaa claims, buildings can "articulate the experiences of our very existence." At most, they can be interpreted that way by some people—and a proponent of aesthetic formalism may respond that the lives of these people would be happier if they learnt to enjoy pure forms independently of any interpretation. Pallasmaa actually classifies as "narcissistic" attempts to value architecture on purely aesthetic grounds and independently of its social role. "The narcissistic eye," he says "views architecture … as an intellectual-artistic game detached from essential mental and societal connections…"[172] This is a value-laden but unsubstantiated dismissal. In his account, architecture should be judged not on its own merit, or its visual-aesthetic qualities, but on the basis of associations one has about it:

> *Alvar Aalto's Paimio Sanatorium is heartbreaking in its radiant belief in a humane future and the success of the societal mission of architecture. Le Corbusier's Villa Savoye makes us believe in the union of reason and beauty, ethics and change, Konstantin Melnikov's Melnikov House in Moscow has stood as a silent witness of the will and utopian spirit that once created it.*[173]

But these are all his own private interpretations. Someone may respond that "narcissism" as a term is more appropriate for an approach that refuses to engage with architectural works in a detached and disinterested way, independent of self-centered personal associations that one projects on architectural works.

CUMULATIVE MODELS OF OBFUSCATION

A more complex strategy of obfuscation consists in combining simple obfuscatory items into larger structures in order to achieve stronger effects.

"*Salads*" are clusters of unrelated (or vaguely related) obfuscatory claims, statements or citations that are placed together in order to achieve a cumulative obfuscatory effect. Some ingredients may appear to argue for the position that the author wants to advocate but are typically inconclusive or only vaguely related to that position. In some cases the author may seem to be adducing the opinions of prominent authors (such as famous philosophers) that support the position, but the existing scholarship on the topic is not taken into account. No effort is made to ascertain the quality of these philosophical positions, the accuracy of the author's interpretation, to respond to possible criticisms (that typically abound in literature) or to take into account alternative interpretations. The position that the salad advocates need not be stated clearly. Although inconclusive, a salad parades the wide erudition of the author.

Consider the introductory chapter of Frampton's *Studies in Tectonic Culture*.[174] The book itself is a serious scholarly study in architectural history and a valuable contribution to the field. At the same time, its opening chapter stands out as a remarkably successful obfuscatory construct that needs to be studied in its own right. It starts with the identification of space as the driving principle behind all architectural form. August Schmarsow formulated this understanding between 1893 and 1914. Frampton points out that Schmarsow's formulation "coincide[d] with the evolving space-time models of the universe as these were successively adduced by Nikolai Lobachevsky, Georg Riemann and Albert Einstein."[175] By relating Schmarsow's work to Lobachevsky's, Riemann's or Einstein's theories Frampton suggests his deeper understanding of the relation between groundbreaking discoveries in different fields. However, Lobachevsky died in 1856, Riemann in 1866, and their work certainly could not have "coincided" with Schmarsow's. It is also utterly unclear (and Frampton does not explain it) what kind of connection could exist between Schmarsow's discussion of architectural space and works of Lobachevsky, Riemann or Einstein beyond the banal fact that they used the word "space" in their work. Instead of providing a clarification, Frampton changes the topic to a discussion of topography that concentrates on the Philopapou walk in Athens designed by Dimitris Pikionis. The walkway, that consists of irregularly coursed pavers bonded into the ground, can be appreciated as an aesthetic object on its own right. Frampton however infers from its rather banal physical features that the walkway "reinterprets the *genius loci* as a mythic narrative, part Byzantine, part pre-Socratic."[176] What this mythic narrative might be and what kind of insight in the local *genius loci* it provides remains unstated, but the sentence suggests that it is something profound. Some pages further Frampton describes the steel frames visible on the side of Peter Behrens's AEG factory in Berlin as "ontologically tectonic."[177] The claim is meaningless—steel frames' "ontology" has nothing to do with their visibility on the façade—but the formulation sounds learned. The discussion then proceeds by a longish citation of Heidegger's discussion of the Germanic concept of *Raum* from "Building, Dwelling, Thinking." Heidegger there asserted that "spaces receive their being from locations and not from 'space'."[178] If height, breadth and depth are abstracted as dimensions, then a manifold that they define is merely extension, Heidegger pointed out. Though further multi-dimensional mathematical manifolds can be abstracted from it, and called "space," they do not contain spaces or places. Heidegger's reasoning is cogent, though it remains unclear why segments of multidimensional spaces could not be mathematically defined as places. However, Frampton then infers that "[t]he implications of this for tectonic are perhaps self-evident, namely the need for human institutions to be integrated with the topography in such a way as to offset the rapacity of development as an end of itself."[179] The problem is that this is simply not what Heidegger is talking about. Additionally, the rapacity of a development is unlikely to have its aim in itself; more likely it is motivated by financial gain. (Arguably, Karl Marx would have much more to say about this than Heidegger.) The discussion is then crowned by another citation from Heidegger, this time from "On the Origin of the Work of Art."[180] Heidegger there states that "temple work … does not make the material disappear, but rather causes it to come forth for the very first time and to come into the Open of the work's world."[181] Frampton does not explain what this might mean, and insofar as the readers do not understand it, but assume that he does (otherwise he would not be citing it), it is fair to expect that they should be impressed. For Frampton, the important insight from Heidegger's essay is that the term "tectonic" relates to Greek term "techne," which means both art and craft. He then infers:

> *This revelatory concept returns us to Vico's verum, ipsum, factum, to that state of affairs in which knowing and making are inextricably linked; to a condition in which techne reveals the ontological status of a thing through the disclosure of its epistemic value.* [182]

If we follow the standard philosophical usage, "ontological status" pertains to the question of whether something is an abstract, material or mental entity. This certainly cannot be revealed by *techne* understood as "art" or "craft." Further on, something that is "epistemic" pertains to knowledge, but what an "epistemic value" might be in this context remains unclear. Even worse, the sentence is poorly structured, since it is unclear whether he is talking about the "epistemic value" of "a thing" or of the "ontological status." (This last criticism is possibly irrelevant because it is motivated by the assumption that the sentence was intended to convey some meaning. This need not be necessarily the case, and he may have been merely motivated by the poetic desire to impress readers by a random combination of philosophical terminology.)

I believe that the concept of a "salad" should be clear by now. The point is not in the obfuscatory qualities of individual segments as ingredients but in their cumulative effect. Concentrated in the opening chapter of the book, these ingredients make stronger impression on the reader than this would have been the case if they were scattered throughout the book. The remaining chapters of Frampton's book actually demonstrate solid scholarship in architectural history (though not quite deprived of bizarre flights of fantasy). The very presence of the opening chapter can be thus seen as somewhat of a mystery: why would someone write a serious book and then preface it with a chapter that significantly undermines its credibility? Why would the MIT Press publish such a book? The only credible response seems to be that from the point of view of the author and the editors, and at the time the book was published (the 1990s) a chapter like this would have *enhanced* the book's credibility.

Cumulative banalities are another cumulative obfuscatory strategy. In this case a large number of banal observations are clustered together in order to give the impression of profound insights. The resulting conglomerate is, one could say, a profound banality on steroids. The approach, that has some grounding in heideggerian rhetoric, relies on a large number of sentences that are clear, trite and comprehensible. Taken together, as Kant described, they are expected to make the public believe that some profound truths are coming in droves behind a series of intellectually barren statements. A good example is Norberg-Schulz's essay "Place and Architecture."[183] The article starts with the observation that natural environment is increasingly destroyed by buildings that are foreign to their places.[184] The humanity is a victim of the loss of place.[185] Our understanding of architecture therefore needs to be revised and the starting point is to understand the phrase "take a place." The article then proceeds by stating a series of platitudes. Here are some highlights:

When something is done or happens, we say that "it takes place." This means that life is tied to places. [186]

But we also need to feel that the environment is "good" or filled with meaning, or to put it briefly, in order to experience that we are "home." Only when this happen can we say that we dwell.[187]

To be tied to a place always means to share it with others. When the qualities of a place open themselves for us we become involved in a community, that also has its history.[188]

When we dwell, we are in peace, protected against danger or injury. In order to achieve such relationship of friendship, we must learn to respect the place.[189]

When we come to a settlement, we leave the environment in order to settle down and create a home. The journey is finished; we have approached the destination. We say therefore that we arrive in the city. The settlement is "in" where life takes place.[190]

When we enter into a house we are finally at home. The home will strengthen our identity and give us safety.[191]

The place can tell us where we are, not by name and various kinds of "data," but because a meaningful characteristic opens itself for us. That way our existence on earth under the sky becomes a defined relationship that gives us foothold.[192]

The recital of banalities that pretend to state profound insights extends for some fifteen pages. The simplicity of Norberg-Schulz's statements should not mislead us to believe that his claims are necessarily true. They are certainly not. It is simply not true that people are safe, protected from danger and injury if they dwell. Their relationship with the place will not protect them if their countries are invaded by an enemy or if the economies of their countries are destroyed by colonialism. Let alone the fact that being a nomad is a legitimate way of life. Through history, for many people, being constantly on the move has been the safest way of life. The apparent simplicity of style thus hides Norberg-Schulz's assumptions and suppresses alternative views instead of taking them into account.

SAVING THE WESTERN CIVILIZATION

An author who wants attention must also advertise his or her ideas as novel and original. It is often necessary to present a widely shared commonplace view as the author's novel insight. For the authors who follow the phenomenological approach, the term "the West" often plays an important role in such self-advertising strategies. It defines the context in (or against which) their groundbreaking insights occur. Consider, as an example, the discussion of the relationship between imagination, thinking and the verbal expression of thoughts in Pallasmaa's *The Embodied Image*.[193] According to Pallasmaa:

"The traditional Western attitude has stubbornly maintained the view that language and thinking are purely incorporeal and disembodied psychological phenomena. According to this attitude, there are tangible material things on the one hand, and disembodied thought, on the other, and thinking is attached solely to our linguistic faculties."[194]

From the point of view of the history of philosophy the claim is not only false, but quite astonishing. An important counter-example is Aristotle (and consequently the Aristotelian tradition including medieval Scholasticism), who clearly separated thinking and language and identified the contents expressed by language with the affections of the body.[195] Thinking cannot be "attached solely to our linguistic faculties" if mental affections are the same for all humans, but languages are not, as Aristotle claims.[196] The belief that language and thinking are purely incorporeal is certainly not a widespread view in the philosophy of mind.[197] It is true that the view that thinking is inseparable from language was actually fashionable for a couple of decades in the second half of the twentieth century, but even then a number of important philosophers rejected it. [198]

Alternatively, the author may argue that "the West" is on the wrong path because of some widespread misconceptions. Typically, these misconceptions are views that originate from the Enlightenment era, and they typically pertain to assumptions about the rational structure of the Universe that underwrite the modern scientific worldview. The author's mission is then to rescue the western civilization by reviving the original, proper understanding of the world (that was typically available to ancient Greeks). The idea of space, as the medium that enables the quantification of sizes (and thus modern physics) is a particularly common target of such efforts, that are not limited to the phenomenological tradition. In his *Changing Ideals in Modern Architecture* Peter Collins thus wrote: "[i]t is a curious fact that until the eighteenth century no architectural treatise ever used the word 'space.'"[199] Patrik Schumacher similarly asserts that "In the world of Classical architecture there was no need for the discourse to descend to the level of abstraction that is implied in the concept of space."[200] In fact, the term "space," *spatium* in Latin, occurs ninety-eight times in Alberti's *De re aedificatoria* from the 1450s. Alberti was certainly aware of the implications of the concept expressed by the term.[201] Norberg-Schulz makes a similar claim that ancient Greek language did not have a word for space.[202] When, in another book, he claims that "[f]or him [Aristotle] space was the sum of all places, a dynamic field with directions and qualitative properties" one is left to wonder how Aristotle could have expressed this view if he did not have a word for "space."[203] In fact, in his *Physics* Aristotle used the Greek word χώρα for space and the word τόπος both in the sense "place" and "space" and explicitly differentiated between these two meanings.[204] Epicurus in his *Letter to Herodotus* lists a number of Greek terms for (empty) space that he suggests are equivalent.[205] Ancient Greeks thus certainly had words for space. In his *Architecture in the Age of Divided Representation* Dalibor Vesely makes a different, but equally bizarre claim about Euclidean space: "Euclidean space was not fully accepted as a structure of the natural world before the seventeenth century, when it became identical with Cartesian space."[206] He does not specify which Euclidean assumptions were regarded as inapplicable to the natural world before the seventeenth century. He certainly could not claim that before he seventeenth century people assumed that nature functioned in accordance with the non-Euclidean geometries that were discovered in the nineteenth century. We should thus disregard Euclid's fifth postulate, that was the main issue in the rise of non-Euclidean geometries. The remaining four postulates say that (a) it is always possible to draw a line from a point to another point, (b) it is possible to delimit a line within a line, (c) it is possible to draw a circle with any center and radius and (d) all right angles are equal. Vesely thus *de facto* claimed that before the seventeenth century people believed that in the physical, natural, world it is impossible to draw a line from any point to any point, or that it is impossible to delimit a line within a line, or to draw a circle with any center and radius or that they believed that right angles were not all the same. Needless to say, he never provided any evidence for his extraordinary claim that invalidates most of the history of science before the seventeenth century as we know it today.

IMPLICATIONS AND MOTIVATIONS

As the earliest stream of the Obfuscatory Turn, phenomenology started to play a major role in architectural discussions in the 1970s. This was precisely the era when the failure of modernist architecture—especially its aesthetic failure—became obvious to everyone, including the general public. It is reasonable to see in the interest in phenomenology and Heidegger an effort to overcome the problem. In the situation when facelessness of glass-and-concrete architecture started to cause widespread dissatisfaction, phenomenology could have seemed to provide a good way to articulate the concerns. It enabled authors who wrote about architecture to express dissatisfaction regarding the cultural role of architecture, human interaction with the built environment, domesticity, place, the adaptation of architectural works to the qualities of their location, and similar. Interest in phenomenology also went hand-in-hand with the rejection of modernists' faith in technology. It is reasonable to think that many people associated the unpleasant aspects of the new glass-and-concrete environments with modern technology.

This explanation of the link between the disappointment in Modernism and the interest in phenomenology has much to recommend itself. Nevertheless, it fails to take into account some important aspects of the phenomenon. It does not actually explain the role that obfuscation came to play in the writings of the proponents of phenomenology in architecture. Obfuscation was a genuine novelty that they pioneered. Nothing similar can be detected in the writings of the proponents of Modernism for the preceding half a century. One may identify the use of obfuscation with a Heideggerian influence, but this does not explain the willingness of architects and academics to endorse this type of influence. People do not just get influenced, by Heidegger or by any other author. Intellectual influences do not spread the same way as viral infections. One *chooses* to be influenced and, for some reason or another, one must be predisposed to do so. In the 1950s, an author who proposed hallucination as a valid tool in our dealing with the built environment could hardly expect to be taken seriously. Some decades later, we have seen, Norberg-Schulz could advocate reliance on hallucinations in forming the built environment and be confident that this would not affect his credibility. It is reasonable to wonder, what were the reasons for, and what interests motivated such a radical revision of intellectual standards?

The belief that the disappointment in modernist architecture brought about interest in phenomenology is also insufficient to explain phenomenologists' anti-visual attitudes. The failure of Modernism largely pertained to its incapacity to provide satisfactory visual experiences. The dissatisfaction of the general public with modernist architecture is typically articulated in terms of its visual ugliness. Modernist urban interventions are regularly criticized because they fail to fit visually with older buildings. Instead of trying to address these issues the authors who advocate phenomenological approaches to architecture tend to play down visual-aesthetic problems by denying the importance (or even the possibility) of purely visual engagement with architectural works. For Norberg-Schulz architectural works are not even perceivable independently of "meanings," *de facto* stories told about them. Perez-Gomez, we have seen, claimed that visuality is constructed by the linguistic context. For Pallasmaa other senses (hearing, touch, smell, taste) are as important as the sense of vision. He even opposes visual concerns as "ocularcentrism." However, the general public is protesting against *visual* ugliness. Hardly anyone is disturbed by the *smell*, let alone the *taste* of modernist architecture. An ugly modernist block remains ugly even if it exudes the smell of a nice perfume. Ugliness does not go away if the architect comes up with a better story about (the "meaning" of) the building he or she has designed. At the same time, it is precisely visual-aesthetic concerns that phenomenologists seek to dismiss. Insofar as dissatisfaction with the visual qualities of the built environment motivates the criticism of modernist architecture, the only solution that they can offer is outright denial of the relevance of visual, formal-aesthetic concerns. It is important to bear in mind these aspects of architects' and architectural academics' endorsement of phenomenology—especially that this endorsement was a strategy of denial. In the Conclusion we shall see that they actually constitute important segments of the wider picture that explains the rise of the Obfuscatory Turn.

DECONSTRUCTION

Some of the greatest works in the history of literature, including books by Goethe, Dostoevsky, Mann and Bulgakov, relate the story of an artist or an intellectual who relied on a demonic force in order to achieve his aims. Versions of the story differ, and Goethe's *Faust* is probably the most widely known. There Mephistopheles introduces himself as the spirit of eternal denial—a well justified attitude, he says, since everything that comes into being should also cease to be.[207] In his view, it would be even better if nothing existed at all, and therefore his proper element is transgression, destruction and everything that humans call "evil." Different authors tell different stories, but, unsurprisingly, such visitations hardly ever end well. The workings of the Evil One tend to be pernicious for those involved. Not, however, in the story that this chapter tells.

In the context of late twentieth-century approaches to the humanities, the eternal denial that Mephistopheles professes sounds uncannily familiar. A similar denial, widely influential in modern times, is Idealism, the view that material reality does not really exist, that it is merely constructed by social, historical, cultural or linguistic forces. A "spirit who always denies," as the demon describes himself, necessarily denies material reality, otherwise he would not be "always" denying. Outside architecture, the wide expansion of idealist (anti-realist) philosophy in various fields of the humanities is normally referred to as Postmodernism. (In architecture this same term means something else, the relaxation of modernist constraints on the use of historically established systems of ornamentation that became fashionable in the late 1970s and the 1980s.) Idealist anti-realism in the English-speaking humanities has often been identified with the influence of French Postmodernism, exemplified in the works of the authors such as Michel Foucault, Jacques Derrida or Jules Deleuze. An important thesis of this chapter is that when it comes to architecture this perspective only covers part of the story. French cultural influence existed, but it was merely an external clothing used to hide the actual concerns and motivations of English-speaking architectural professionals and academics. The roots of Idealism in architecture were much older and deeper.

THE FRENCH ARE INNOCENT...

The claim that French sources exercised only marginal influence on English-speaking architects and architectural theorists in the final decades of the twentieth century is going to raise some eyebrows. To be sure, authors such as Derrida, Deleuze or Foucault were extensively cited and numerous doctoral students wrote dissertations that related their work to architecture. For more than a decade, completely benign and innocent undergraduate architecture students were regularly assaulted by tutors who ranted incomprehensible phrases about the presence of absence and architecture as a form of writing. One should not, however, confuse parading verbal behavior for the intentions and anxieties that it concealed. In the case of architecture academics, for instance, the failure to manifest such behavior would have seriously affected one's career prospects. At the same time, there are (at least) two important arguments against the widespread opinion that French intellectual influence played a major role in the architectural trends of the 1980s and the 1990s. The first is the incomprehensibility of the texts of French postmodernists. It is impossible to be influenced by texts one does not understand. The mechanical repetition of other people's phrases does not count as *intellectual* influence. Writings of Derrida or Deleuze, for instance, are notoriously obscure and difficult to understand even for specialists. The idea that practicing architects or architectural academics could have understood much of their content is ludicrous. Maybe these texts actually do have some coherent content (this is certainly debatable and many analytic philosophers would deny it) but that content is so inaccessible that it cannot be a platform of a widespread architectural movement like Deconstruction of the 1980s and the 1990s. The second argument is that the main tenets of the worldview that motivated architects who endorsed (what they called) Deconstruction in architecture were well-known and can be documented in the intellectual life of English-speaking countries well before Derrida, Deleuze or Foucault wrote their most influential books. To be sure, when they talked about their architectural works, deconstructivist architects did talk about texts, absences and presences in ways that resemble French philosophers of the era. They used the same jargon. Nevertheless, reading Derrida, Foucault or Deleuze will not get us very far if we want to understand the architecture of the last decades of the twentieth century. Rather, in order to understand it, we need to take into account a version of the romantic idealist worldview, more radical than the one we have seen in the previous chapter. In any case, it is important to bear in mind that the word "Deconstruction" can mean two things: what Derrida meant by the term and what some English-speaking architects and academics meant, and that these two meanings are very likely to differ.

The view that Derrida's influence on Deconstruction in architecture was not more than a smokescreen is surprising only until we try to *specify* this influence. Jeffrey Kipnis's first-hand account of Peter Eisenman's attempts to collaborate with Derrida does not suggest that their interaction had relevance for Eisenman's design.[208] In Kipnis's description it seemed "as if an obsessed Eisenman wanted nothing from Derrida but an endorsement of scaling," one of Eisenman's design procedures.[209] Subsequently, in his "Letter to Peter Eisenman" Derrida did all he could to distance himself from (what he described as) Eisenman's excessive belief in absence. Short of an insulting affront, Derrida's letter reads as clear rejection of Eisenman's views. Admittedly, as Robin Evans described some years before the event, within the rules of the game of American East Coast avant-garde it is hard to avoid unwilling complicity because "opposition becomes just another species of affirmation."[210] It is, however, undeniable that Derrida rejected Eisenman's endorsement of "absence," whatever this latter term, crucial in the writings of both Derrida and Eisenman, might mean.

The fundamental problem of the view that French postmodernists influenced deconstructivist architects' designs (and not merely their verbal behavior) lies in the difficulty to establish what that influence might be. One would have to be able to state (for instance) what Derrida's views on architecture were, and then show their relevance for architects' design decisions. However, consider the following statements by Derrida in his discussion of Bernard Tschumi's La Villette project:

Maintenant [now]: if the word still designates what happens, has just happened, promises to happen to architecture as well as through architecture, this imminence of the just (just happens, just happened, is just about to happen) no longer lets itself be inscribed in the ordered sequence of a history: it is not a fashion, a period or an era.[211]

This could be interpreted to mean that things that happen now still do not belong to history. He then continues:

On the one hand, [if this happens to us] it does not happen to a constituted us, to a human subjectivity whose essence would be arrested and would then find itself affected by the history of this thing called architecture. We appear ourselves only through an experience of spacing which is already marked by architecture. What happens through architecture both constructs and instructs us. The latter finds itself engaged by architecture before it becomes the subject of it: master and possessor. On the other hand, the imminence of what happens to us maintenant [now] announces not only an architectural event but, more particularly, a writing of space, a mode of spacing which makes a place for the event.[212]

It is impossible to say what this might mean. Derrida is talking about something he calls "the essence of human subjectivity" whose "now" (from the sentence cited above) is not arrested by the history of architecture. Whether human subjectivity has essence and what this might be is unclear. He also claims that something he calls "an experience of spacing" is necessary for us to appear to ourselves and that we are constructed and instructed by things that happen through architecture. (The nature of this construction and instruction is unexplained. He does not say whether construction/instruction happens only through architecture nor whether what happens through architecture always constructs/instructs us.) He further submits that architecture engages instruction before instruction becomes its subject. How instruction can be the subject of architecture remains unclear. The final sentence then talks about "a writing of space" which is "a mode of spacing which makes a place for the event." This is allegedly announced to us by the imminence of what happens now.

It is not our topic here to evaluate the philosophical merit of insights like these, the way it was not in the discussion of Heidegger's impact on the writings of architectural phenomenologists. This is a controversial issue among philosophers. Among analytic philosophers, for instance, Derrida's reputation is probably even worse than Heidegger's.[213] The same as in the case of Heidegger, some readers of this book may chose to agree with analytic philosophers and further infer that Derrida's followers among architects and architectural academics of the 1980s and the 1990s were imposters. For the same reasons that were described in the previous chapter, this view can be only marginally relevant for our discussion here. Nevertheless, it is unavoidable to ask about the motivations of those architects and theorists who spent a lot of energy to understand texts similar to the one cited above. What could motivate someone to seek to understand, and even pretend to have understood, an author who makes no effort to be comprehensible and obviously does not want to be understood?

It is certainly significant that if we try to establish *the content* of the possible influence of French postmodernist authors on architects and architectural theorists during the era, we run against a wall. Consider, for instance, John Rajchman's discussion of Deleuze's significance for Eisenman's work.[214] Deleuze differs from Venturi and Rowe, Rajchman says, because Venturi operated with the notion of contradictory whole, and Rowe with cubist collage and Gestalt perception. For this reason their approaches result in liberal-minded "toleration of ambiguity" and they come to oppose "revolutionary-minded rationalist promise of a new order."[215] Admittedly, one can see how this, or something similar, could be said about Venturi and Rowe. But then Rajchman provides the following insight:

> By contrast, Deleuze's conception of complexity-in-divergence leads to the Question; it leads to the practical ethic of not being unworthy of what is disturbing the spaces we inhabit—of this Other who is knocking at our door.[216]

We are never told what the "Question" is, who is this "Other" how one can be "unworthy of what is disturbing the places we inhabit." After this impressive and unexplained claim Rajchman comes to explain the concept of "perplications." These are "'cross-foldings' that introduce a creative distantiation into the midst of things."[217] They are

> foldings that expose an intensive multiple complexity in the fabric of things rather than a contradictory framed one; they unearth 'within' a space the complications that take the space 'outside' itself, or its frame, and fold it again.[218]

Such complexity for Deleuze, Rajchman further explains, is always virtual.

But such virtuality cannot be a dynamis any more than such actuality can be an energeia; for otherwise complexity would reduce to the unity of pregiven origins and ends. 'Intensity' is rather a nondynamic energy; and actuality always occurs in the midst of things, just as virtuality is always to be found in intervals.[219]

"Dynamis" (δύναμις) in Greek means "strength, might, power" whereas "energeia" (ἐνέργεια) means "action, operation." Both terms play an important role in Aristotelian philosophy, but it is not clear that Aristotle has any relevance for the account of Deleuze's influence on Eisenman. Insofar as Rajchman's explanation of Deleuze's influence on Eisenman has no content—and it is hard to find some content in what he says—it is fair to conclude from his description that there was no influence at all, at least as far as he can explain it.

CONSEQUENCES OF IDEALISM

In the previous chapter we have seen that romantic Idealism played an important role in the worldview of those architects and theorists who endorsed phenomenological approaches to architecture. By the 1980s and the 1990s idealist views became dominant in numerous fields of the humanities in the form of various anti-realist and social-constructionist agendas. This increased influence of idealist philosophy coincides with the era when English-speaking scholarship was dominated by the generation of academics born immediately after World War Two—the same generation that, as students, stood behind the events of 1968. What came to be known as "Deconstruction" in architecture relied on the idealist worldview whose core premises were available in English in the 1960s and the early 1970s, before the works of French postmodernists.

The implications of Idealism are best explained if one compares them with those of the materialist (physicalist) perspective that Idealism rejects. The materialist view is that the material world is a given, that it is not constructed by social phenomena such as cultures or languages. Typically, it is assumed that mental states are ultimately biological, that all biological phenomena are chemical and all chemical phenomena ultimately result from the physics of subatomic particles. Social phenomena (cultures, languages and so on) result from interactions between biological human individuals. They are not something over and above human individuals and their interactions. They cannot influence the beliefs and the worldview of individuals independently of these individuals' interactions with other individuals. They certainly cannot construct the physical reality in which humans live. For architecture this means that there can be no communal spirits, spirits of places, or forces such as *Zeitgeist*. At the same time, the biological nature of human cognition also makes it plausible that humans derive pleasure in reaction to certain shapes, colors and their combinations, independently of the ideas that they associate with them. As we have seen in the first chapter, this allows the possibility that there could exist culture-independent forms of pleasure that are derived from architectural works.

Materialism of this kind seeks to be in line with modern science, or at least not to contradict it. In the 1950s and the 1960s (as described in the second chapter) the materialist worldview was heavily undermined by "New Look" psychology and the belief that the contents of human perception *always* depend on the way we classify and conceptualize the things we perceive. Modern psychology rejects this view, but (as described in the previous chapter) the view was dominant in mid-20th century psychological research. It also exercised a massive impact on the humanities during the 1960s. The view makes it difficult to treat the material world as simply given. If *all* perception depends on what we believe about the objects we perceive, or how we classify them, then it cannot provide us with a direct access to the physical reality. That access is then always pre-affected by our beliefs and classificatory capacities. One version of this view would be to assume that our perception is determined by our previous individual experiences, but that the material world nevertheless exists on its own. For instance, Gombrich's view was that the way artists see the physical reality depends on their previous experiences and beliefs, but the physical reality is still there, unaffected by what they may think.[220] What artists think can be affected by their social environment, but this environment consists of physical human individuals and their interactions. The problem with this view is that it is not clear how we can know about the existence of the physical reality once we accept that our perception results from what we know, expect or believe—that perception itself has no independent relation to reality. Constructionism, as a version of Idealism, is based on the rejection of such attempts to combine the view that all seeing is seeing-as with the view that the material world is still a given. Instead, it assumes that physical reality has no existence on its own, but that it is constructed by cultures, languages, history, social-historical contexts and so on, and that these forces that construct it have independent, immaterial existence. Rather than being caused by human interactions in the material reality, they are seen as the forces that generate that reality. From this point of view, the existence of biological human individuals (as well as the belief that they exist) is not a given. Instead, it is likely to be seen as a cultural construct, a mere a product of individualist beliefs typical for western cultures. A good example of such strong Idealism is Norman Bryson's criticism of Gombrich's view that the physical reality that artists imitate remains the same through history. In Bryson's view, history constructs reality itself.[221] The version of the idealist worldview that became influential during the 1980s and the 1990s was not a novel idea and it was not a result of French influence. As mentioned, the view that all seeing depends on what we believe is normally associated with American New Look psychology of the 1950s. Even before that, as early as the 1920s, the Gestalt psychologist Kurt Koffka claimed that we perceive a diesel engine differently once an engineer explains us how it functions—that our perception is constructed by what we know.[222] Similarly, the idea that the physical reality that artists imitate remains the same—that it is unaffected by spiritual developments—was rejected by the Viennese art historian Hans Sedlmayr as early as 1927.[223]

EXAMPLES OF CONSTRUCTIONISM

It is useful to consider here some examples of constructionist positions from different fields of the humanities in order to understand the implications of this view for architecture. In the philosophy of history, for instance, there exists a long-standing debate about the view that historical past did not really happen and that it is merely constructed by historians.[224] An influential view is Leon Goldstein's position that the truth of historical statements is merely a result of the agreement within the community of historians.[225] According to Goldstein, statements about historical past are not true because they accurately describe events that happened. Rather, they are true because historians agree that they are true. Historians' agreement constructs what happened in the past. This agreement, he claimed, is not justified by some independent criteria. Instead:

> *For whatever reasons, some historical constructions will seem to the community of scholars better than others that have*

been proposed, and these latter will simply be dropped from
consideration.[226]

The implication is that the view of the majority of historians can never be false. Their agreement constructs what happened in the past by making sentences about the past true or false. For many people, the view is counterintuitive in the extreme.[227] The community of historians may be, for instance, controlled by a totalitarian political system, or influenced by ideological prejudices or rabid nationalism. There is no reason to assume that the majority of historians always get it right. Such criticism seems cogent, but it assumes that events in the past indeed happened and that historians merely describe them. If this were so, then it could indeed happen that the majority of historians acquire false beliefs about some past event. This criticism of Goldstein's position will not work if one assumes that the past did not happen, but that it is merely something historians write and agree about, "for whatever reasons," as he puts it. (It's a bit like the proof that we should always trust the mainstream media. How do we know that the mainstream media always tell the truth? Because truth *is* what the mainstream media report.)

Similar social Constructionism motivates institutional theories of art developed by analytic philosophers such as George Dickie or Arthur Danto in the 1960s and the 1970s. Dickie's definition of a work of art says that it is "… an artifact … upon which some society or some sub-group of a society has conferred the status of candidate for appreciation."[228] It follows that the actual properties of the object itself, the properties that the object has independently of the social context, such as shapes and colors, are irrelevant for its status as an artwork. For instance, Dickie says,

> *The Field Natural History Museum in Chicago recently exhibited*
> *some chimpanzee paintings. In the case of these paintings we*
> *must say that they are not works of art. However, if they had*
> *been exhibited a few miles away at the Chicago Art Institute*
> *they would have been works of art.*[229]

In other words, no intrinsic properties of an object—properties that the object has on its own, independently of its social environment—contribute to its status as an artwork. In fact, insofar as it is presumed that perception is determined by classification, and classification dependent on the social context, these properties could not be even perceived independently of the social interactions in which the object participates. There can be no intrinsic properties—they are always already constructed by social forces. The same applies, presumably, to architectural works as well. Again, this view will be counterintuitive to many people. One may, for instance, consider what would happen if this reasoning were applied to other fields. It would follow, for instance, that a person has toothache not because of the pain in a tooth, but because dentists say so. The biological state of the tooth or what the person feels would be irrelevant. More precisely, the equivalent view would be that the biological state of the tooth does not even exist independently of the social context—that it is constructed by the opinions of dentists.

Idealist commitments, implied or explicitly stated, permeate the writings of deconstructivist architects and theorists. Peter Eisenman, for instance, fully endorses the view that our vision is determined by the ideas we associate with the things we see. He states that "we do not see a window without relating it to an idea of window" or that "the column is always already embodied with meaning."[230] If someone took a modern-day student to see Mies's Barcelona Pavilion, Eisenman claims, the training, culture and discourses that the student has been exposed to would prevent him or her from seeing the building the way Mies saw it in 1929.[231] Eisenman has often been attributed strong formalist positions, but his is not *aesthetic* formalism. In his view it is not even possible to engage with shapes and colors independently of the ideas one associates with these shapes. In a way similar to Goldstein, he claims that "truth is a managed item developed by committees, produced by writers, and sold by media spokesmen."[232] (Note that he is talking about *truth* and not merely people's *beliefs*.) He also claims that "[t]ruth changes in the course of history. History is a force which changes the notion of what is true at any one time."[233] Aesthetic values, in his view, are also socially constructed. One and the same object such as Marcel Duchamp's urinal, can acquire aesthetic properties as a result of the change of its social context.[234] In other words, one and the same urinal can be placed in a toilet or in an artistic exhibition—and in the latter case its aesthetic qualities will be bestowed on it externally, by the context itself. Its own properties that do not depend on the social context, such as shapes and colors, are irrelevant.

In the case of architecture, Constructionism implies that there are no specific qualities that belong to buildings and make them good architecture or even architecture. Rather, it is the agreement of architects, especially the "leading" architects, the "avant-garde," that decides about (constructs) their status as architectural works. The situation is not different from the way the agreement of the community of historians, according to Goldstein, constructs the historical past. In Goldstein's account, a person counts as a historian because other historians recognize him or her as one of them. Similarly, in the case of architecture, it would follow that there are no specific skills or knowledge that would make a person an architect. Rather, he or she is admitted in the profession because his or her acting is recognized by other members of the profession as that of an architect. This correlates to the belief, common in the 1990s, that architectural education does not provide students with specific skills or knowledge but with enculturation into the profession.[235] For instance, in the social environment of Sydney architects, an architect's standing can be enhanced by good sailing skills and the ability to do well in the Architects' Annual Boat Race.[236] Those individuals who exemplify the appropriate behavior will be considered as the avant-garde. The background assumption is that everything constantly changes and that architects should always endorse the direction of the change. They should never resist it. They should always blindly follow "where things are going." Some architects are better at anticipating the direction of change and they count as the avant-garde. How can we know who belongs to the avant-garde? Obviously, this is decided by other members of the avant-garde. In Goldstein's model, a historian is not trying to establish what happened in the past but seeks to write historical works that other historians will approve of. Similarly, from this point of view, an architect's aim is not a building that will be aesthetically, structurally or functionally successful. Rather, an architect should seek to achieve a building that other architects, especially the avant-garde, will approve of. The same applies to texts about architecture. Texts by deconstructivist architects are not meant to advocate ways to build more functional, structurally sound or more beautiful buildings. Rather, they seek to achieve the approval of the avant-garde and establish or confirm the author as one of its members. For a young architect or an architecture academic in the 1990s this could have been a survival issue.

Romantic Idealism and the Glory of Absence

It would be futile to try to understand the intentions and the aims of architects and theorists who preached Deconstruction in the 1980s and the 1990s if one overlooks their (one is tempted to say, fanatical) commitment to constructionist Idealism and their faith in the pronouncements of the avant-garde. The important problem with Deconstruction is that it is not easy to say why one would want to introduce it into architecture or what is gained by doing so. The question "Why" weighs heavily on discussions of the projects of deconstructivist architects. In his introductory essay to the catalogue of the exhibition in the New York Museum of Modern Art (that established Deconstruction as the dominant style of the next decade) Mark Wigley described deconstructivist architecture as marked by "disruption, dislocation, deflection, deviation, and distortion."[237] A deconstructivist work, he says "produces a feeling of unease, or disquiet."[238] The projects presented at the exhibition, he further explained, activate "some part of the context to disturb the rest of it, drawing out previously unnoticed disruptive properties."[239] "This is not freedom, liberation, but stress; not release, but greater tension."[240] "The nightmare of deconstructivist architecture inhabits the unconscious of pure form rather than the unconscious of the architect."[241] The curious aspect of Wigley's "Introduction" is that his enthusiastic endorsement of the works he selected for the exhibition reads as a condemnation that borders on being insulting. It is incomprehensible why one would want to collect and exhibit architectural works such as he described. Bernard Tschumi's discussion of his own works assumes the same tone. He says that they "have no beginnings and no ends. They are operations comprised of repetitions, distortions, superpositions, and so forth. ... The idea of order is constantly questioned, challenged, pushed to the edge."[242] His Parc de la Villette project, he says, "rejected context," and "can be seen to encourage conflict over synthesis, fragmentation over unity, madness and play over careful management."[243] Remarkably, this is not meant to be self-criticism. Tschumi seems to be proud of what he has done. In Eisenman's writings too, such seemingly depreciating statements about one's own work are not rare and do not imply self-criticism. For instance, the "autonomous architecture" that he hoped to achieve in his early houses "would necessarily create anxiety and a distance, for it would no longer be under man's control."[244] A reader who does not take into account the all-powerful role attributed to the avant-garde can only be puzzled about the aims Wigley, Tschumi and Eisenman describe. Who would want such architecture? Do such buildings count as architecture at all? From deconstructivists' perspective these are the wrong questions to ask. There is nothing good or bad, right or wrong, beyond the judgment of the avant-garde. (This is equivalent to Goldstein's thesis that there is no historical past, but only the agreement of historians.) The avant-garde decides what kind of verbal behavior is to be endorsed in the moment. The writings of Wigley, Tschumi and Eisenman certainly exemplify the verbal behavior that was desirable during the era, since we know that these statements were received as avant-garde statements. For the same reason it would be quite wrong to complain, for instance, that Wigley in his discussion of how to translate deconstruction into architecture never explains why one would want to do it in the first place.[245] Eisenman similarly provides litanies of demands of what architecture must do and we are never told why. In order to become more like a sign, he says, architecture must reduce its opacity; it must confront and dislocate the perception that it is about reality, authenticity, and genuine truth; in order to "dislocate dwelling, architecture must continually reinvent itself"; architecture must resist tendency to create institutions; "[i]t must dislocate without destroying its own being, that is, it must maintain its own metaphysic."[246] It is pointless to ask why architecture should do any of this, or even how. Often, it is not even clear what his demands might mean. Rather, such sentences are acts of verbal behavior that he could expect that they would be received with approval by the avant-garde. The reception of his writings shows that he was right about it. It would be quite wrong to think that something good or bad would be achieved or missed if architecture did or did not heed Eisenman's demands. But it could have been bad for his avant-garde status had he produced some different sentences.

The avoidance of formal-aesthetic concerns is a particularly conspicuous aspect of the writings of the advocates of Deconstruction in the 1980s and the 1990s. The move clearly relates to the avant-garde's endorsement of words such as disruption, dislocation, deflection, deviation, distortion, disruption, disorder, disarrangement, destabilization, dehiscence. If these words express what is valued in architectural works, this could not be compatible with the concern for beauty, harmony, elegance or similar. The background motivation for this theoretical move will only become clear in the Conclusion of this book. As for now, one needs to note that this suppression of aesthetic concerns occurred in an era when problems with architecture-generated aesthetic pollution of the urban environment were widely known and discussed. In an interview in 1987 Eisenman stated that his work "suggests that there is no such thing as the good or the beautiful. The beautiful contains the ugly, the good contains error etc."[247] Considering the time when the statement was made, it is hard not to wonder whether it reflects the lack of confidence in one's own ability to engage with aesthetic issues. Similarly, his statement that architecture "consists simultaneously of signification, function, and objecthood" is clearly intended to oppose Vitruvius's view that architecture consists of utility, firmity and beauty or Palladio's triad of commodity, perpetuity and beauty.[248] One is certainly entitled to ask what happened with formal-aesthetic concerns in the redefinition of the discipline that he proposed. Why was beauty unmentioned? What is the motivation for such silent suppression of visual, formal-aesthetic issues? He may think that beauty is irrelevant, but it would be necessary to explain why. Furtive attempts to avoid the topic can hardly convince anyone. One similarly has the right to smell a rat when Tschumi says that for centuries architects have been haunted by the question of whether "the functional and technical characteristics of a house or a temple [were] the means to an end that excluded those very characteristics?"[249] In other words, in his view, their dilemma has been whether there may be something in architecture that is over and above function and structure. It is hard to believe that Tschumi has accidentally overlooked that architects have been also motivated by formal-aesthetic concerns. One unavoidably wonders about the agenda, and possibly denials, that motivate these omissions.

The suppression of aesthetic issues and the desperate efforts to avoid the topic are so persistent in the writings of deconstructivist authors that one cannot fail to notice them. The phenomenon even leads to grotesque misrepresentations in their discussions of architectural history. Deconstructivists may have had their reasons to think, or to try to show, that beauty, elegance or harmony are irrelevant or impossible. This does not justify, however, the attribution of the same view to architects from the past. In Eisenman's essay "The End of the Classical" formal-aesthetic issues are an elephant in the room whose presence he desperately seeks to avoid mentioning. We are told that classical architecture is marked by three concerns ("fictions," as Eisenman calls them) "they are *representation, reason,* and *history.*"[250]

The idea that, for instance, Renaissance architects may have been motivated by formal-aesthetic issues is utterly suppressed through the essay. Eisenman thus claims, "Renaissance buildings, ... received their value by representing an already valued architecture,"[251] and that Jacopo Sansovino's use of the classical orders on the Library of St Mark "speaks not to the function or type of the library, but rather to the representation of a previous architecture."[252] However, Sansovino could have been motivated by formal, visual and aesthetic concerns. His architecture need not speak to anything. For Eisenman's interpretation to work, he would have to show that during the Renaissance, mere use of Roman architectural elements, without any aesthetic merit, would have been regarded as satisfactory. We know that this was not the case because Palladio himself testifies that Sansovino was praised for *la bella maniera*.[253] He does not mention that Sansovino was praised for the representation of previous architecture. In another essay Eisenman reduced Alberti's design of the façade of San Andrea in Mantua to a combination of a triumphal arch and a temple front. [254] The analysis completely suppresses visual, formal and aesthetic issues that Alberti had to struggle with in the design. There are numerous ways to combine a triumphal arch and a temple front in a single façade, but only some compositions are aesthetically successful. Proportioning and visually adjusting the ornamental elements so that they visually fit each other would have been a very complex task.

The suppression of functional concerns is another important implication of constructionist Idealism in architecture. Eisenman in particular has often been targeted by his critics for his attitude towards functional issues. This criticism, however, overlooks the constructionist perspective on the problem of function. Eisenman's critics assume the existence of human beings as biological creatures with biological needs. The criticism also assumes that these needs define the functional requirements of architectural works. In other words, the idea is that architectural works have to be designed so that biological humans can use them. However, insofar as our culture, language, context, the avant-garde, and so on structure or construct our reality, human beings can hardly be more than mere constructs. In the modern era, Eisenman says, the human being

> is no longer viewed as an originating agent. Objects are seen as
> ideas independent of man. In this context, man is a discursive

function among complex and already-formed systems of language, which he witnesses but does not constitute.[255]

To summarize: in Eisenman's view, objects are but ideas and humans are discursive functions. From the point of view of such radical Idealism architectural works indeed cannot have functional requirements. If we accept that human beings are discursive functions they cannot have biological needs or physical presence. Consequently it will be impossible to specify the functional requirements that a building needs to fulfill. Discursive functions, for instance, do not need doors or windows.

It certainly makes little sense to criticize the works of idealist ("deconstructivist") architects by starting from the assumptions that they reject. Nevertheless, one must notice that the credibility of these assumptions *in our modern time* is questionable. Contrary to what Eisenman says, in our modern times objects *are not* seen as *ideas* independent of man. The very belief in the existence of ideas independent of man is not modern. It is Plato's. Modern scientific worldview does not regard objects as ideas but takes them to be clusters of physical particles. It is equally unclear why we should take human beings to be "discursive functions" (nor what this means) rather than biological organisms. Similarly, the standard view in our modern era is not that languages exist on their own, but that they result from the biology of the human brain. Without biological brains there are no languages. Once these points are noted, one has to wonder about the motivations that could make the idealist worldview attractive to architects in our time. How could such an improbable ideology come to dominate the architectural profession in the final decades of the twentieth century? The medical profession, for instance, never surrendered to the claim that diseases or human biology are merely cultural constructs. Medical schools never accepted the view that their main job is the enculturation of students in the profession. So, why did architectural profession endorse (or seemed to endorse) this view? Why precisely in the final decades of the twentieth century? These questions have to be left for the final section of this book.

THE RHETORIC OF OBFUSCATION

It is important to differentiate between phenomenologists' and deconstructivists' endorsement of romantic Idealism. Both sides relied on the assumption that contextual forces such as culture or language construct the physical reality. Phenomenologists, however, did not postulate the avant-garde as the ultimate arbiter of what is right or wrong, true or false. As a result, phenomenologists and deconstructivists substantially differ in their use of obfuscation. Phenomenologists were still inspired by the desire to improve the quality of the built environment. More precisely, they wanted to show that their anti-visual, romantic approach would make things better, and amend for the problems generated by Modernism. Insofar as they relied on obfuscation, its aim was to legitimize the views they advocated. They believed that they were doing something good that would make human lives better. Deconstructivists, however, aimed for the approval of (what they regarded as) the avant-garde. The belief that architects should improve the environment, from this point of view, would be relevant only insofar as the avant-garde endorsed it (which was not the case). It would be quite inappropriate, and even unfair, to judge deconstructivists' views by their potential contribution to the ways architecture affects human lives. Instead, the aim of their statements, writings and theorizing was to show that they individually belong to the avant-garde. This could not to be achieved by proposing ways to improve the human built environment, but by combining words in avant-garde-like ways in one's writings. It should be added that in addition to words, and combinations of words, their texts or parts of their texts very often also have contents, though this is not mandatory. Contents are used when the author wants to acquire or sustain the avant-garde status by expressing the views appropriate for an avant-garde author. Deconstructivists' use of obfuscation is therefore differently motivated than it was the case with phenomenologist authors. Nevertheless, the typology of obfuscation presented earlier in this book still holds, except that profound banalities are rare in deconstructivists' writings. This indicates that they are less influenced by Heideggerian rhetoric, and that they tend to follow French rhetorical models instead. Also, their use of obfuscation often has more radical forms.

A fine example of *obfuscation plain and simple*, for instance, is Wigley's statement:

> *Just as writing is necessarily exceeded by the sense of spatiality it might exemplify, the subversive quality of that spatiality is frozen whenever it is treated as a "concept."*[256]

This elegant sentence states that while writing exemplifies the sense of spatiality, this sense exceeds writing. If we treat this spatiality as a "concept," Wigley says, this will freeze its subversive quality. It would be quite improper to ask how space could have "subversive quality," how it could be treated as a "concept," or how "the sense of spatiality" can "exemplify" the writing that "exceeds" it. For a historian, the fact that Wigley fails to provide an explanation testifies that such clarifications would have been unwelcomed by the avant-garde of the era. It is thus inappropriate to expect them. It is also unlikely that they would be possible at all. Insofar as the aim is to generate acts of verbal behavior that would be approved of by the avant-garde, it is not necessary to produce meaningful sentences.

Eisenman himself, as a particularly prolific author, well versed with the workings of the avant-garde, provides numerous finely polished examples. Consider the following gems from his essay "Misreading Peter Eisenman":

> As every dislocation of presence also requires, to some extent, its reaffirmation, any activity that would entirely abandon the terms of both the metaphysic and the physic would not be involved in the activity of dislocation but of destruction, for dislocation is enabled only by the play of absence against presence, by the work on and within the contradictory terms of discourse.[257]

> Even as any architecture shelters, functions, and conveys aesthetic meaning, a dislocating architecture must struggle against celebrating, or symbolizing these activities; it must dislocate its own meaning. Dislocation involves shifting but not obliterating the boundaries of meaning, and since meaning necessarily implies absence through the absent referent, then a dislocating architecture must be at once presence and absence.[258]

> The resurfacing of absence implied or contained within presence can be called the dislocating text of architecture. Conventional architecture suppresses absence by creating histories of absolute presence through the suppression of architecture's intrinsic absence, thus centering the experience of architecture in the object.[259]

It would be pointless to ask whether the "reaffirmation" in the first paragraph pertains to "dislocation" or "presence," or how dislocation can shift but not obliterate the boundaries of meaning. It would be equally pointless to remind that words often refer to present things and that meaning therefore does not necessarily imply absence. One is certainly not expected to inquire about the meaning of phrases such as "the suppression of architecture's intrinsic absence." Nor should one ask how Eisenman knows what "architecture's intrinsic absence" might be. (Does this "intrinsic absence" have four legs? Is it made of blue cheese? Does it grow on the Moon? If not, how can one know?) Such questions would indicate the inappropriate expectation that these paragraphs should be meaningful. Again, this need not be the case, insofar as their aim is to combine words and phrases in ways that would be approved of by other members of the avant-garde.

Daniel Liebeskind's article "Fishing from the Pavement" certainly ranks among the finest jewels of this kind of literary production. Consider the opening paragraph:

> Sedition is rooted in education which only appears to equal the whistle—sound dissolving the face's angry citadel.

> A fully equipped talent is attuned to the sea. Rum for sketchy farewells, static abbatoir [sic]. I am praising the city by spilling six phantoms on show of evident docility.

> —Taste excess with your cranium or advise the togaed attacker stranded on an oriental amphora that tall Saxons float in shame, ring shaped columns do not bend, Ghenghis [sic] Khan ridicules restrictions—Are you entranced by fourteen hundred theorems, a dappled rabbit, cows bleating in the attic, ineffable apples? After all the Universal Savant is airborne on the back of a billion Sibyls who shape cameos for few cents while flying. As for repair in the loving eruption, open scissors. I think of drinking diorite: testing a pedestrian conundrum with theatrical homocide [sic].[260]

The article came out in a 1990 issue of the *Journal of Philosophy and the Visual Arts* dedicated to philosophy and architecture. It continues for fourteen pages of insights such as those cited above. Readers who are not acquainted with the underlying assumptions about the avant-garde may even feel uncomfortable reading it. There are psychological conditions in which people write texts of this kind and it may be pointed out that one should have sympathy for people who suffer from such conditions. Compassionate readers might thus actually reproach the editor (Andrew Benjamin) for publishing the article. They may think it unkind to expose in public an author's psychological condition in this way. However, there should be no doubt that the editor (who made extensive contributions to the theoretical discussions of the era) knew what he was doing. He certainly recognized that the article was in line with the views of the avant-garde. It tells much about the era, the editor, academic publishing and the avant-garde that the article was not merely included in the volume, but published on special paper and with enlarged fonts. The editor clearly recognized in it a major contribution to the field.

Pretentious falsities in their simple and traditional form are merely false statements that make a certain type of impression on the readers. But this does not apply the works of deconstructivist authors. In this case it is the avant-garde that decides what is true or false and what kind of claims are to be approved of. It may happen that some claims by avant-garde authors appear to be false, inaccurate or self-contradictory. But this merely means that the reader who thinks so has not achieved the capacity to appreciate the avant-garde skills in combining words. (It's a bit like the clothes made by weavers in Hans Christian Andersen's "The Emperor's New Clothes": whoever could not see the clothes, the weavers explained to the Emperor, must be unusually stupid.[261]) This means that in the case of deconstructivist authors, pretentious falsities are not really falsities but merely appear to be so to less sophisticated readers. Consider the following claims made by Tschumi:

> *Remember: with Descartes ended the Aristotelian tradition according to which space and time were 'categories' that enabled the classification of 'sensory knowledge.' Space became absolute. … Returning to the old notion of category, Kant described space as neither matter nor the set of objective relations between things but as an ideal internal structure, an a priori consciousness, and instrument of knowledge.[262]*

An unsophisticated reader, a historian of philosophy who has no access to the profound teachings of the avant-garde for instance, could be quite critical about this paragraph. He or she may point out here that location (where, "ποῦ") is indeed one of Aristotle's ten categories, but location is not the same as space.[263] Such a reader may further insist that, famously, Aristotle denied the existence of space.[264] Lacking sophistication, this reader may further complain that it is not clear in what sense space "became" absolute with Descartes. (In what sense, for instance, Epicurus's conception of space was not "absolute?") The reader may even be so crude as to point out that space is simply not one of Kant's twelve categories.[265] If this unsophisticated reader has inclination towards analytic philosophy he or she may further insist that the claim that space is "an ideal internal structure" is meaningless and certainly not Kant's: something can be internal or external only within space, so it makes no sense to say that space itself is internal. Such criticism relies on the assumption that there are facts (for instance, about the views of old philosophers) that can be true independently of what the avant-garde says about them. This assumption is something that deconstructivists reject. Rather, Tschumi's statements are to be appreciated because he combines words such as "Descartes," "Kant," "space," "categories" in an avant-garde way.

Unsophisticated readers may also think that they have encountered a pretentious falsity when the views of a deconstructivist author seem counterintuitive. Wigley, for instance, cites Derrida's view that the opposition between an infrastructure and a superstructure cannot be taken for guaranteed when deconstructive analysis enters. He infers from this that

> In such displacements of the traditional architectural
> figure, structure is no longer simply grounding through a
> continuous vertical hierarchy from ground to ornament, but a
> discontinuous and convoluted like an enigmatic series of folds.
> At the very least, the building is no longer simply standing on
> the ground, and the whole conceptual economy it is meant to
> put in place is disturbed.[266]

It may be pointed out that unless a building is floating in the air (arguably a rare phenomenon) it must stand on the ground. Someone might therefore think that the idea of a building without ground is simply nonsense. However, one should appreciate it as a novel and original idea that demonstrates the avant-garde status of Wigley's views.

It may also happen that unsophisticated readers find the claims of deconstructivist authors self-refuting. Tschumi, for instance, observes that cultural or commercial programs have ceased to be determinate, since they change all the time. He then continues:

> *There is no causal relationship between buildings and their content, their use, and of course, their very improbable meaning. Space and its usage are two opposed notions that exclude one another, generating an endless array of uncertainties.*[267]

A reader who lacks the necessary sophistication to appreciate the statement may protest here that there can be no usage of space without space. However, the fact that Tschumi can conceive of the usage of space without space is a convincing proof that he is a legitimate member of the avant-garde.

The use of the *jargon of profundity* always reflects the associations that people in a certain context have with profundity. In the era dominated by the worldviews of the student generation of 1968, this meant showing that one is opposed to the establishment. (The fact that at the time they were writing many of these authors *were* the academic establishment is of marginal significance.) In such a context, expressing a view, an affirmative statement, is always dangerous. Texts abound with "…is not," "cannot," "is never" "does not" sentences. Here is one example, from Wigley:

> *Deconstructive discourse can never be detached from architecture. It can never be extracted from what it destabilizes. … It is not a drifter that simply occupies and dislodges an architecture before moving on. It is never singular, never just one coherent discourse and, furthermore, each of its multiple discourses is itself divided, occupied even, by the very architecture they seem to inhabit and disturb.*[268]

It is very dangerous for a deconstructivist author to say what something is, because that opens the door to accusations for superficiality. In the era dominated by the spirit of denial, saying what something is not suggests profound thoughts, while saying what something is suggests a dogmatic mindset. Similarly, one rarely reads in the writings of deconstructivists that they seek to preserve, save, defend something existing. (As Mephistopheles put it, it would be better if nothing came into being in the first place.) Rather, favorite verbs, accompanied by approval are "subvert," "inhibit," "exploit hidden resources or contradictions," "prevent completion," "defer," "frustrate," "displace" and so on. "Dis"-words abound.

Cumulative models of obfuscation reach new levels of complexity in the works of deconstructivist authors. In the case of phenomenologists, we were still dealing with authors who had a point to make. They had views about the built environment and they used obfuscation in order to advocate these views. Deconstructivists' ambitions, however, concentrate on the affirmation of one's avant-garde status. They operate within a different paradigm in which their texts are validated as texts, as combinations of sentences intended to achieve the approval of the avant-garde, often independently of the content they might (but need not) convey. Consider, for instance, the opening section of Andrew Benjamin's Introduction to his *Architectural Philosophy*. His claim is that

> the possibility of experimentation and therefore the possibility
> of alterity and criticality within architecture depends upon
> retaining particularity as the site of activity. What this
> means is that the locus of the critical and thus the domain
> of experimentation are ultimately linked to creating other
> possibilities within and for function.[269]

The hopeful reader may think that this is an unnecessarily complicated way to say that function must still be there when novelties are introduced in architecture. This interpretation is further confirmed by the statement:

> Function, it will be argued, cannot be thought outside a
> complex structure of repetition. Function is given within, and
> as, forms of repetition.[270]

Possibly, this means that an architectural work can be used many times with the same function. But the hope of learning something about Benjamin's architectural philosophy dissipates very soon, already on the next page, when one reads:

> Rather than allowing for a prescriptive or didactic conception
> of criticism, the primordiality of repetition means that alterity
> how to figure with the possibility of a repetition that takes
> again for the first time.[271]

And further:

*Built in to the move to alterity is both the inscription of a level
of unpredictability though equally a level where function is
retained.[272]*

These sentences are from the first two paragraphs of the
Introduction to the book. Presumably, they explain to prospective
readers what the book is about. The very opening paragraphs of
Benjamin's book illustrate how wrong it would be to attribute to
him the desire that people read what he has to say. He is certainly
not guilty of the populist tendency to write clearly nor interested in
making his views accessible to readers. He not trying to impose his
views on other people. Nor is he trying to entice the reader to continue
reading. Rather, the book illustrates his (well-informed) beliefs about
the kinds of word-combinations that would ensure him the status of
an avant-garde author.

THE MEANINGLESS MEANING OF ARCHITECTURE

A particularly surprising aspect of the writings of the advocates of
Deconstruction is their claim that they have discovered that meanings
of texts, art- and architectural works ("works" as Kipnis calls them) are
undecidable. Kipnis actually describes this reinvention of the wheel as
"perhaps the most difficult and virulent aspect of deconstruction."[273]
Here is what he says about the view that Deconstruction presumably
debunks:

*Every work—written, spoken, performed, drawn, or built—is
considered to be decidable in principle, that is, to have an
ultimate reason, explanation, meaning, or finite set of meanings
(hereafter referred to collectively as 'meaning') that could be
fully exposed and comprehended.[274]*

We are never told who endorsed this view.[275] Since the view that
deconstructivists claim to refute is profoundly counter-intuitive, it
is hard to imagine that many people ever thought so. Certainly, in
the case of many books one normally differentiates between various
interpretations that result in different meanings. It is, after all, an
old interpretative principle of medieval Scholastic philosophy that
everything that is received can only be received (i.e. understood and
interpreted) in accordance with the recipient, *ad modum recipientis*.[276]
Interpretations by various readers will unavoidably differ from the

author's intention. Even the claim that the author's intention should determine the correct interpretation makes sense only insofar as one admits that different interpretations are possible. Interpretations massively depend on what readers know and the questions they ask when they approach a work. It should be normal that in many cases these interpretations cannot be "exposed and comprehended" as Kipnis puts it.

It is, however, the use of "have" in the above paragraph that one should be careful about. It implies that works somehow *have*, possess, meanings on their own, that their meanings are not merely attributed to them by various individuals. While deconstructivists reject the claim that these meanings are definite, the implicit suggestion is that they still assume that things can have meanings independently of how one understands them. The rest of the article indicates that Kipnis indeed thinks that meanings, reference and similar linguistic phenomena somehow exist independently of linguistic groups, society and the biology of the human brains. Reference, the relationship between words and things they are about, plays a particularly important role in his account. Kipnis claims that "the conditions of reference in general" exist on their own, independently of the social conditions that generate languages.[277] They are, he says, "primordial and essential, anterior to any thing, origin, or ground."[278] The next important step in the argument is the claim that everything that can be referred to can also refer to something else. For instance, my words about a black cat refer to the cat, but the black cat itself can be taken to refer to bad luck. (He thus assumes that words refer on their own; the alternative view that it is people who attribute reference to words or black cats is completely absent from his account.) Kipnis then infers two claims:

> Every "thing," therefore, is constructed as a "thing" in a field of reference. Before there can be meaning as proper reference there must be reference in general.

The first thesis is the standard idealist thesis of linguistic Constructionism. It is similar to Perez-Gomez's claim, discussed in the previous chapter, that "[t]he verb 'to see' was reciprocal in Greek; whoever saw was seen, and the blind were invisible."[279] The assumption is that the way words refer to things decides the way things are. Obviously, it can be responded that things can exist if nobody refers to them, if they are not "in the field of reference." There is no reason why we should accept Kipnis's claim that things exist only insofar they are talked and written about—that is, referred to. It is perfectly reasonable to think that there are physical things, and that some of them are biological creatures such as human beings. Reference would then be the relationship between the words that humans use and the things these words are about. Without human biology, there can be no linguistic reference. Contrary to this view, Kipnis's second sentence in the above paragraph asserts the existence of something that he calls "reference in general." The conditions for its existence are, as mentioned, "primordial and essential, anterior to any thing, origin, or ground."[280] Without it, even physical things would not exist, he implies. Again, it is not clear why we should accept that there is such a thing. One should, however, note that Kipnis's views of language are not unlike the views of various mystical traditions that postulated the Word, *Logos*, or similar linguistic phenomena as the force that underwrites the existence of the physical Universe.

These same assumptions about meanings that border on mysticism underlie Eisenman's struggles against the (improbable) view that architectural works have firmly established meanings. We have seen that Norberg-Schulz believed that architectural meanings pre-exist buildings and that architects merely discover them. Eisenman seems to endorse a similar view and then spends an inordinate amount of energy trying to suppress these meanings in his design work. He thus states that in his Houses I and II the aim was "to free house of acculturated meaning whether traditional or modern."[281] The concerns that motivate his efforts are incomprehensible if one assumes that meanings, signs, representation, are merely attributed to architectural works by some people and that other people may disagree with these attributions. If one assumes that meanings in architecture are but associations that some individuals have and other people need not share, Eisenman's concerns make little sense. His efforts to deconstruct these meanings become both bizarre and pointless. (How can one prevent people from having associations with the buildings they see? How can one predict the associations that various people will have in order to deconstruct them?) Consider his statement that "[a]rchitecture has always assumed that like language and like art, it has signs, i.e., that figuration is representational."[282] The response is that this may be true of some authors. As mentioned in the first chapter, an important part of the classical tradition—authors such as Alberti, Palladio or Guarini—were concerned with beauty that, according to their definitions, depended on relationships between parts. They did not assume that beauty depended on associations people may or may not have with architectural works. Eisenman also claims that since architecture manifests its presence in physical reality, "[an architectural] work is a sign of physical reality."[283] However, no thing by itself is a sign of anything. People take it as a sign of something or they do not. Some people may regard architecture as the sign of physical reality, others may not. (I don't.) In the case of the modernist reduction of ornamentation, Eisenman says, "[t]he 'abstract' column referred, albeit negatively, to the tradition of columns," it was "still a sign of something else to be decoded by an observing subject."[284] But columns could not refer to something without someone taking them to refer to something—and even if some people would take them to refer others probably would not.

Starting from this perspective on meanings, Eisenman then seeks to suppress or deconstruct them. As mentioned, it is hard to see the purpose in these efforts if one thinks that architectural meanings are merely associations various people have with buildings. In Eisenman's view, the physical nature of built architecture suggests the promise of reality, authenticity, and genuine truth.[285] Again, this may be the case for some people, but not for others. Many people would deny that there is anything authentic or genuine (except possibly blandness and ugliness) about modernist corporate architecture. Only if we accept Eisenman's assumption, however, can we follow him in his next step. Here too, if one does not take into account that he is presenting avant-garde-member-appropriate combinations of words one can only be surprised by the claims he makes in order to justify his designs. He asserts that architecture is defined by "the continuous dislocation of dwelling," by the dislocation of "what it in fact locates" and that "the status quo of dwelling does not define architecture."[286] We are left to wonder why we should accept these assumptions. This is certainly not obvious, and he offers no convincing arguments. Nevertheless, we can count on him to be right about the kind of view the avant-garde is likely to endorse. Similarly, his early houses, he says, were intended

> to dislocate the house from that comforting metaphysic and symbolism of shelter in order to initiate a search for those possibilities of dwelling that may have been repressed by that metaphysic. ... While a house today still must shelter, it does not need to symbolize or romanticize its sheltering function; to the contrary, such symbols are today meaningless and merely nostalgic.[287]

In order to see this as a problem, one must first assume that architectural works have fixed and determined meanings and symbolism that pertains to shelter. If different people associate different ideas with buildings, he would be seeking to repress something that only some people care about. Thus, when he infers: "… in a world of irresolvable anxiety, the meaning and form of shelter must be different"[288] we are left to wonder why different people could not associate different forms with the idea of shelter. Eisenman's statements appear as poorly justified theoretical claims if we do not take into account the need to coordinate explanations of his design with the types of verbal behavior endorsed by the avant-garde. Consider, for instance the claim (cited above) that architecture is defined by "the continuous dislocation of dwelling." Let us accept that this is so, even though no justification has been provided for the claim. Why is he then not deconstructing this very "dislocation?" Why is "dislocation" exempted from being deconstructed? Similarly, "ugliness," "relativism" or "commercialism" are much likelier candidates for the meaning of much of late-twentieth-century architecture than the promise of reality, authenticity, and genuine truth. So why is he not seeking to dislocate ugliness, relativism or commercialism from contemporary architecture? The refusal to consider such alternative views demonstrates once again the seriousness of his commitment to the regime of the avant-garde.

"WE HAUNT THOSE WHO HAUNT US"

The failure of Derrida's collaboration with Eisenman is an important illustration of the incompatibility of Derrida's views with their reception by American East Coast intelligentsia. Admittedly, in a cultural context so deeply committed to Idealism, Derrida's views, whatever they may have been, would have been irrelevant. The only thing that mattered was that his combinations of words could be recycled by individual protagonists for the purpose of presenting oneself as an avant-garde thinker or architect. With his reputation as an impenetrable philosopher, Derrida provided a great resource for promotion strategies of many academics and ambitious architects of the era. He was certainly someone to be associated with, considering his reputation as the great spirit of denial, deconstruction, the promoter of the absence of presence, the modern way of saying that it would be better if nothing came to be. It is a question for specialists in his philosophy to decide whether this perception of Derrida was accurate.

There should be no doubt that American East Coast intelligentsia (and especially theoretically minded architects) expected from him an endorsement of their brand of Idealism. Derrida's own reactions and statements must have therefore sounded disturbing to Eisenman from the beginning of their collaboration, had he cared. (He need not have. From the moment their collaboration started, whatever Derrida said, however vehemently he disagreed, could only enhance Eisenman's avant-garde status.) Very early in their collaboration Derrida warned Eisenman that absence, however profound, is still what it is—that is, nothing. [289] Kipnis, who witnessed and described the collaboration between Derrida and Eisenman, provided an extensive account of Derrida's architectural conservatism.[290] Its most conspicuous aspect was, he says, "a certain suspect voice he gave to public responsibility and the inviolability of domesticity."[291] Derrida, indeed, went so far as to recommend to Eisenman to discuss poverty, social housing and homelessness.[292] Both Eisenman and Kipnis complained about his unwillingness to accept in architecture the same discomforting techniques that he abundantly practiced in his writing.[293] One has to sympathize with their bewilderment. Social responsibility, after all, is a form of good will. How could Derrida, who dismissed Hans-Georg Gadamer's statements about good will because in his view they referred to "unfindable objects of thought" expect architects to have good will towards their clients and people using their buildings?[294] One is reminded here of the old adage about (many) French intellectuals— that they don't mean what they preach. As Czeslaw Milosz grasped decades before Derrida wrote his first works, their revolt against the bourgeoisie

> ...conceal[s] a certain respect for order, and they would have quaked had someone told them that if they carried their rebellion to its conclusion, it would mean no more little bakeries, no more package-goods stores or bistros with their cats dozing in the sun behind windowpane. Theirs was always a secure revolt because their bitterness and their nihilism rested on the tacit understanding that ... thought, even the most violent, did not offend custom.[295]

"[S]omeone told them..."—this is indeed what happened. Eisenman did it. He presented the architectural implications of deconstruction to Derrida, and Derrida *quaked*. Derrida actually expected, Eisenman reported later with bewilderment, that parks should have benches and trees.[296] Clearly, benches imply the existence of human beings who would sit on benches. This would further require the existence of biological humans who participate in the physical reality. Voicing public responsibility means suggesting ethical obligations, and ethical obligations make sense only if people have biological existence, if they are not discursive functions. One can have ethical responsibilities to real people, not to discursive functions. And by assuming the inviolability of domesticity, Derrida, the world-famous philosopher of eternal denial, came to accept the presence of real bistro cats and to defend their right to doze in the sun.

We are thus facing here a drama of cosmic proportions that takes us beyond *Faust* to something much bigger. In order to illustrate the full scale of the event and its consequences for the Universe, it is necessary to abandon the history of real characters (such as Eisenman or Derrida). They are biological humans and therefore unsuitable; we are talking here about demons and architects who can engage with them. This would have to be a literary work about ideal types—an epic that Goethe could not conceive of, whose psychology Dostoevsky could not explain and whose absurdity Bulgakov would be hesitant to put on paper. The demonic force that, world literature informs us, in the past tormented German professors and composers, Russian tsarist-era intellectuals and Stalin-era writers, arrives to New York to haunt an American deconstructivist architect. But the haunting backfires. Forget about Goethe, Dostoevsky, Mann or Bulgakov. The ordeal turns out to be more like MTV's series *Teenwolf*. The motto of werewolf hunters in the series is "we hunt those who hunt us." Similarly, our epic describes, in New York there are architects who haunt those who haunt them. The demon thus gets haunted by the architect, whom he originally planned to haunt. He sees himself in the architect as a reflection of nothing in an absent mirror. The absence of absence, the demon comes to realize, does not add up to presence. (Similarly, we shall see in the Conclusion of this book, the ignorance of ignorance does not amount to knowledge.) Horrified by the abyss of the absent absence that the architect has designed, the demon dis-displaces himself back to Paris, back to the domesticity of fat bistro-window cats. As the airplane takes him home where he will be firmly rooted in the presence of talking about absence, he shouts his endorsement of Being and Presence over the roofs of Manhattan: "I believe in the extreme! *Hosanna in excelsis!*" Architecture can sometimes achieve miracles.

THE ABYSS

"Absolute Reason has died last night, at 11 PM. ... this is quite regrettable," announces Professor Begriffenfeldt, PhD, the director of a Cairo lunatic asylum, in the fourth act of Henrik Ibsen's *Peer Gynt*.[297] For a director of a lunatic asylum the death of Absolute Reason must be a disturbing affair. For the readers of this history, the citation signifies the moment when it becomes necessary to turn to Ibsen in order to illustrate what has happened with architecture since the 1990s. Goethe, Dostoevsky, Bulgakov or Mann, we have seen, would help us as long the story deals with an architect tempted and haunted by a force that celebrates nothingness. But we are now beyond temptations or haunting. The depth of the Fall that interests us here is the one in which even the Devil has abandoned the architect. Since we are still talking about imaginary, literary characters, the architect's situation is comparable to that of aged Peer Gynt who returns to Norway after many years abroad. In his youth, before he left, the king of trolls explained to him the difference between humans and trolls. For humans, the highest law is to be themselves; for trolls it is to be *enough* for themselves. The meaning of this "enough" is revealed only in the final act, when Peer Gynt encounters Death, in the form of a button molder. Gynt, it turns out, has been a troll all his life without knowing it. He is scheduled to be melted and recycled, like a metal button, for only those who were themselves can remain what they are when they depart to Heaven or Hell. Those who sought "enough" remain in between, as nothings in the endless process of recycling. Seeking "enough" means seeking and never having enough of external correlations, such as recognition, fame, money, power, love and similar. Eventually, the person becomes defined by, reduced to and nothing more than these external relations, the newer and newer roles that one plays in order to follow "where things are going" and to achieve this "enough." Roles and correlations take over and there is no independent self left. Hell—let alone Heaven—would not take such a nullity. (Demons, we have seen, escape back to Paris when they encounter it.) It is reasonable to assume that what applies to humans and trolls applies to architects as well, and to the architecture they design. If we remove all social, public, professional, academic roles that an architect plays in relation to his or her architecture, is there something left? Is there something left in an architect's efforts and designs if we disregard social posturing, stories, narratives, meanings, philosophical pretense that he or she sells to the clients, colleagues, academics, the general public? To ask the same question using Richard Rorty's metaphor: if we remove vines from the façade of a house, is there a house behind the vine, or do we merely find another layer of vine?[298]

DEMISE OF CONTINENTAL PHILOSOPHY

Ibsen is, however, not only insightful but also prophetic, insofar as we are talking about the era of the 1990s. The point is not merely that some readers may take the lunatic asylum in Cairo as an appropriate metaphor for the architectural theorizing that we have witnessed in the preceding chapters. When he talks about the death of Absolute Reason Ibsen does not mean *human* reason. It would be hard for human reason to die, since it is a hard-wired capacity of human brains. As long as there are biological humans, human reason will necessarily be there as well. Ibsen's commentators explain that by Absolute Reason Ibsen meant the German (in our terms here, continental) philosophy of his time.[299] Continental philosophy, including German, that underwrote the Obfuscatory Turn in the final decades of the twentieth century indeed died in the 1990s. The last generation of influential French thinkers, for instance, Derrida, Foucault or Deleuze left no prominent successors. Those contemporary philosophers who continue to follow the old continental models of doing philosophy are marginal figures: their texts are hardly ever found in major philosophical journals or published by established publishers. Typically, they do not have positions in leading philosophy departments. It is quite possible that a major reason for the demise of continental approaches to philosophy was the introduction of double-blind refereeing by academic publishers. "Double-blind refereeing" means that after the author submits a manuscript to a journal or a book publisher, the editor passes it to experts in the field who evaluate it. The identity of the author remains unknown to the reviewers and the identity of reviewers is unknown to the author. This model has dominated English-language academic publishing for a very long time; in continental Europe, it has been introduced only in recent decades. Its introduction coincided with the demise of continental-style approaches to philosophical work. The method seeks to ensure merit-based selection of manuscripts for publication and to eliminate academic patronage. The academic models developed in continental Europe over centuries, however, were precisely based on academic patronage—a system whereby a professor would promote careers of his or her doctoral students or assistants by providing them with the contacts that would enable them to publish their works or find academic appointments. In philosophy, patronage-based academic models often result in scholarship that is less concerned with logical rigor or the quality of arguments and much more with the presentation of grand claims. Such scholarship often strives to impress important professors or the wider academic community, rather than experts in the field. Authors are under pressure to sound profound and obfuscation is often the most efficient way to produce this impression. At the same time, the academic model in which texts are selected for publication on the basis of independent experts' opinions emphasizes logical rigor, suppresses the flights of fantasy or grandiloquent claims. The pressure is to look competent, rather than profound. It is inconceivable that texts such as Heidegger's discussions of "Fourfold" (mentioned in Chapter Two) could pass the independent, double-blind refereeing process of modern philosophy journals. Once their authors are unknown, and manuscripts are evaluated exclusively on their argumentational merit, obfuscation becomes the kiss of death.

Since architectural theory during the twentieth century systematically relied on stimuli from the works of continental philosophers, the demise of continental philosophy dramatically changed the field of operation. We have seen that Walter Gropius and Mies van der Rohe relied on spiritualist speculations of German historicist philosophers, Norberg-Schulz on Heidegger-style phenomenology, Wigley and Eisenman on Derrida—in all these cases approaches to architectural theory claimed credibility on the basis of their association with philosophical works published in recent decades. It was the association with the famous brand-new Continental philosopher that mattered. In his discussion of the translation of deconstruction into architecture Wigley complained that Derrida was introduced "into architectural discourse" "over twenty years" after his first books were published.[300] In order to jump on the bandwagon of the latest avant-garde philosophical celebrity, one also has to recognize that celebrity. However, in the first decade of the twenty-first century, no famous continental philosophers could be found to provide an avant-garde bandwagon and legitimize contemporary architectural theory. Continental philosophy was dead by the end of the preceding century. Even if old masters such as Heidegger, Derrida or Deleuze had something valuable to contribute today, one could hardly legitimize this contribution as something new. In the wider philosophical perspective, the dominance of analytic philosophy further reduced the philosophical credibility, and consequently the relevance, of the old masters of continental philosophy. When a contemporary architectural theorist writes that Derrida was "the most seminal philosopher" of the 1970s, he is either nostalgic or uninformed.[301] Anyone who checks the syllabi of contemporary philosophy departments will see that the most influential philosophical texts of that decade were works of analytic philosophers: Saul Kripke's *Naming and Necessity*, Hilary Putnam's "The Meaning of Meaning" and Tyler Burge's "Individualism and the Mental."[302] It would be hard to find a fourth philosophical text of the 1970s that is read and discussed more by contemporary philosophers or philosophy students. In contemporary philosophy departments, courses that discuss Derrida are rare. At the same time, works of analytic philosophers are not easy to mine for phrases, citations and unusual ideas that could be used in order to legitimize design approaches or theoretical positions. Philosophical credibility founded on arguments and logical technicalities necessarily results in high levels of specialization. As a social system, contemporary analytic philosophy consists of hundreds of philosophy departments across the globe in which thousands of analytic philosophers busily construct their own arguments, gleefully refute the arguments of their colleagues and respond to the refutations of their old arguments. The game seems to have no end, and developing the ability to engage in it requires years of work. One needs to know whether arguments one presents may have been refuted in the past and how these refutations could have been responded to—and to know this, one needs to master a massive amount of specialist literature.

Consider two examples by authors whose theorizing is discussed later in this chapter. In his *Autopoiesis of Architecture* Patrik Schumacher claimed that the attribution of aesthetic properties such as beautiful or ugly to architectural works is inseparable from their stylistic classification.[303] This is the view, for instance, that we attribute aesthetic properties to Gothic buildings as Gothic buildings, as buildings from a certain era. In analytic aesthetics, this view was argued by Kendall Walton in his 1970 paper "Categories of Art."[304] At that time, it was commonly believed, and Walton could implicitly assume, that all perception is inherently dependent of classifications. Insofar as things could not be perceived without being classified, it was reasonable to state that the attribution of aesthetic properties also always depends on classification.[305] By the late 1990s, the dominant understanding of human perception changed, and Nick Zangwill was able to point out that Walton's reasoning was based on unjustified generalizations. Zangwill argued that there is no reason why one should not be able attribute some aesthetic properties to objects independently of how one classifies them.[306] At the present moment, there is no conclusive argument that would show that the attribution of aesthetic properties depends on classification, stylistic or otherwise. From the point of view of analytic aesthetics, Schumacher's is a five-decades old claim that was refuted more than a decade before he made it.

Another similar example is Graham Harman's argument against "undermining." Harman calls "undermining" the idea that entities (things, buildings, social institutions) are mere sums of their parts, that they are nothing more than the particles that make them up.[307] His argument against undermining is that an object remains the same even when its parts change, get replaced or simply disappear. For instance, a hammer can lose a couple thousand atoms and still remain the same hammer—therefore we should not identify it with the sum of the atoms that make it up.[308] Similarly, the fleet of the Dutch East India Company was an object on its own, and not an aggregate of ships, since over time it lost some ships, acquired new ones, without ceasing to exist.[309] According to Harman, objects *emerge* as distinct from the sum of their components.[310] In the philosophy of the social sciences this old argument has been known at least since the 1930s, and it is known that it does not work.[311] To assume that things are always sums of their constituting parts does not mean to assume that every single thing is always *one* single sum of its parts. Saying that the fleet of Dutch East India Company was different sets of ships at different times, does not oblige us to admit that it was something else, over and above these ships. Rather, it was different sets of ships at different times. There is no need to say that something immaterial emerged out of the set of ships. Rather, we use one and the same phrase to refer to different sets of ships at different times. Similarly, if a hammer looses a couple thousand atoms, it will become a different set of atoms, but that does not mean that it will cease to be a set of atoms.

Paradigms and their Contemporaneity

The gradual disappearance of continental philosophy as a source of new paradigms in architectural theory came to be felt by the late 1990s. For a period of time, during the 1990s, it still seemed that Gilles Deleuze's work could provide ways to fill the gap. Deleuze wrote a number of texts about philosophers such as Spinoza and Leibniz. Because of the high obfuscatory quality of Deleuze's own work, it became legitimate and fashionable to invoke Leibniz (and sometimes Spinoza) in architectural writings. We shall consider an example of this approach in the next section. It leads to similar problems as attempts to engage with works of analytics philosophers. The works of older philosophers often require that one deals with arguments and reads the existing scholarship. At the same time, however complex the arguments of these philosophers may be, few of them produced texts with sufficient obfuscatory qualities that could be successfully mined for impressive phrases and citations. They do not provide suitable material in order to bamboozle one's readers. The tendency to see the fabrication of obfuscatory texts as a legitimate job of a philosopher is a particular aspect of twentieth-century continental philosophy. Finally, invoking philosophers from the past requires one to explain the reasons for choosing to talk, for instance, about Kant and not Aquinas. It becomes impossible justify the choice by saying that a certain philosopher is the latest fashion in Paris. (Deleuze's authority merely provided a brief reassurance in the case of of Leibniz or Spinoza.)

A careful reading of works on architectural theory at the turn of the century indicates desperation that resulted from the increasingly meager diet that continental philosophy was providing for architectural theorists. A collection of texts on architectural theory from the period 1993-2009 edited by Krista Sykes illustrates the doubts that arose from the lack of philosophical avant-garde bandwagon.[312] A substantial number of papers that Sykes included in the collection sought to articulate a position against "criticality"—a term used to refer to approaches associated with Michael Hays and Peter Eisenman that had been dominant in the preceding decades. Typical criticisms pointed out that "disciplinarity has been absorbed and exhausted by the project of criticality,"[313] that "theoretical vanguards had none of the political or philosophical *gravitas* of their early twentieth-century predecessors,"[314] that "theoretically inspired vanguards ... operated in a state of perpetual critique ... incapacitated by their own resolute negativity,"[315] that architecture "ceases to be 'cool' when it clings to the critical tradition."[316] At the same time, the opponents of criticality were seen as failing to "deliver an actual, affirmative project," or to be able to state a credible alternative.[317] In other words, the philosophical justifications on which Hays, Eisenman and their followers relied lost their luster, but new philosophical narratives were not coming from European continental philosophy in order to take their place. Obviously, this had to happen in a situation when contemporary philosophical production failed to provide material that could be mined for new theoretical approaches. "The architecture community is now left to face the future without guidance from the all-knowing theory vanguards that dominated schools since the 1970s," Michael Speaks observed in an article in 2005.[318]

A heroic attempt to save the situation was proposed by John Rajchman in his 1998 article "A New Pragmatism." [319] Rajchman's proposal was to revive more than hundred years old philosophy of American pragmatism as the base of architectural theorizing in the twenty-first century. A famous line in Tomasi di Lampedusa's novel *The Leopard* says that everything must change so that everything could stay the same. Rajchman's proposal was in line with a more cogent assumption that nothing relevant should change so nothing would have to change. The unstated background insight of his proposal seems to have been that contents of incomprehensible sentences are mutually indistinguishable. Consequently, one could keep writing the way one did in the preceding decades—it was enough to rename this new approach "pragmatism" as opposed to "deconstruction," and one could continue playing the same game. Nobody will be able to tell the difference anyhow. Additionally, a reference to a genuinely American philosophical movement is also intellectually democratic since it removes the elitist requirement to learn foreign languages in order to engage with works of non-English speaking philosophers.

In the article mentioned, Rajchman defines as "diagrammatic" "those images or spaces that introduce other 'possible movements' not predetermined by an overall program."[320] We then get told that

> *The diagrammatic dimension thus helps free an older idea of*
> *'function' from absorption or negation by a purist aestheticism*

while undoing its identification with the preprogrammed stories or sets of interrelations.[321]

This probably means that by talking about diagrams one can avoid the dismissal of functional concerns in favor of aesthetics or narratives associated with function. He further explains that

The diagrammatic supposes a pragmatic relation to a future that is not futuristic, not imaginistic. It is concerned in the present with those multiple unknown futures which have no image just because we are in the process of becoming or inventing them.[322]

These sentences seem to be an impressive way to say that what is unpredictable cannot be known in advance. He then concludes that the "pragmatism of diagram"

might help move beyond the impasses of older images of negative theology, transgression, or abstract purity and introduce a new problem: that of resingularizing environments, of living an indefinite "complexity," prior to set determinations, which questions the simplicities and generalities of our modes of being and suggests other possibilities.[323]

Although it is hard to say what it might mean, the sentence is certainly a masterpiece.

Rajchman's proposal ultimately, however, produced only a limited impact. In 2000 there were a couple of events dedicated to it.[324] One can imagine that participants at such events respectfully and enthusiastically exchanged similar artistically-crafted sentences with each other. Sykes notes that "despite the fanfare surrounding these occasions, talk about pragmatism had largely faded out within a few years."[325] This is hardly surprising. The demise of continental philosophy left a vacuum that was not easily filled by giving an old and venerable name to the well-known ways of generating sentences in architectural theory.

GEOMETRY STRIKES BACK

The introduction of computers in architectural practice during the 1990s radically changed the pool of interests of practicing architects and the questions that architectural theory needed to address.

Unlike the commercially-imposed domination of modernism during the late 1940s and 1950s, this was a genuine revolution, driven by a genuine breakthrough in technology. The revolution affected the ways architects design, communicate and document their designs. It enabled the generation and documentation of formal systems that were unavailable to architectural practice in the past. The renewal of interest in geometry also implied an increased commitment to intellectual rigor, clarity and the avoidance of obfuscation. At the same time, the delay in the rejection of obfuscation-based models of theorizing shows the strength of the models of legitimization that became established in architectural theory during the 1980s. Greg Lynn's writings of the era are a good example. In order to make his point, Lynn should not have needed obfuscation at all: he was arguing for (and managed to bring about) the change of style from deconstruction to smooth shapes. He also pioneered many aspects of the use computers. He made genuine and groundbreaking contributions to the field of architecture itself. Nevertheless, his writings of the era are not lacking in grandiloquent formulations. One can only infer that in the atmosphere in which he was writing, he needed to make such statements in order to legitimize himself as part of the avant-garde. For instance, the sentence:

In the Statue of Liberty, the architectural quality (other than firmness or structure) that distinguishes the colossus from sculpture is an aleatory commodiousness within the interior.[326]

is a way to say that the Statue counts as architectural work because it has some spaces inside that can be used by people. It is not clear whether Lynn was merely paying lip service to French postmodernists or genuinely found it difficult to step out of the mold. In spite of his emphasis on visual aspects of architecture, he still insisted that architecture is a form of writing.[327] He actually endorsed Luce Irigaray's curious views on the mechanics of fluids (that were subsequently mocked by physicists such as Alan Sokal and Jean Bricmont).[328] Admittedly, he was facing a difficult challenge. His mathematical interests could have been seen as logocentric (a mortal sin in the eyes of the avant-garde). He needed to package them in order to make them palatable for the followers of French postmodernists. The term "anexact" that he introduced from Derrida's discussion of Husserl, for instance, certainly helped to avoid this inculpation.

Deleuze's book on Leibniz was a major tool in Lynn's efforts to legitimize his mathematical interests in the eyes of the avant-garde.

It should be mentioned that the book has no standing in scholarship about Leibniz. It is, for instance, not cited in bibliographies of scholarly works on Leibniz such as *Stanford Encyclopedia of Philosophy* nor discussed in surveys of modern scholarship on Leibniz such as the *Cambridge Companion to Leibniz*.[329] Arguably, this is not surprising, since Deleuze himself did not engage with contemporary research and debates about Leibniz nor did he present systematic analyses of texts. A historian of philosophy could hardly take Deleuze's book as a relevant contribution to the field. One important reason is that it is often impossible to understand what Deleuze is saying, or what kind of view he is attributing to Leibniz. Consider, for instance, the following sentence:

> *The living organism, ... by virtue of preformation has an internal destiny that makes it move from fold to fold, or that makes machines from machines all the way to infinity.*[330]

Deleuze's discussions of Leibniz's mathematics belong to the same obfuscatory genre, including the discussion of folds that Lynn relied on. The physicists Sokal and Bricmont, who analyzed mathematical claims in Deleuze's works in general, have found "a great concentration of scientific terms, employed out of context and without any apparent logic, at least if one attributes to these terms their usual scientific meanings."[331] They talk about an "avalanche of ill-digested scientific (and pseudo-scientific) jargon."[332] Examples are not missing in Deleuze's book on Leibniz. Deleuze, for instance, considers an isoscale right-angled triangle with a hypotenuse AB and the point C opposing it.[333] It is possible to draw a circle with a center in A and radius AC so that it cuts the hypotenuse. The ratio between the length of the hypotenuse and the segment thus created is an irrational number, $\sqrt{2}$. This is meant to illustrate his point that:

> *The irrational number implies the descent of a circular arc on the straight line of rational points, and exposes the latter as a false infinity, a simple undefinite that includes an infinity of lacunae; that is why the continuous is a labyrinth that cannot be represented by a straight line. The straight line always has to be intermingled with curved lines. a point fold.*[334]

What a "false infinity" or "a simple undefinite" might be remains unexplained. As we have seen in earlier chapters, such undefined phrases incapacitate criticism and suggest the profundity of thoughts that the author is presenting. However, in this case (possibly because we are dealing with a mathematical example) obfuscation fails to hide the fact that Deleuze's claim is false. All his example describes are two lines that stand in an incommensurable ratio. It certainly does not show, as he claims, that every straight is "intermingled" with curved lines. Deleuze further claims:

The arc of the circle resembles a branch of inflection, an element of the labyrinth, that from an irrational number, at the meeting of the curved and straight lines, produces a point fold.[335]

The fold is Power, as we see in the irrational number that appears by way of an extraction from a root, and in the differential quotient that appears by way of the relation of a magnitude and a power, as a condition of variation.[336]

These claims are irrefutable because they are meaningless. This meaninglessness also explains the lack of architects' interest in scholarship on Leibniz beyond Deleuze. Considering extensive references to Leibniz in architectural discussions of the era one would expect that some architects at least would consider wider scholarship, possibly learn Latin in order to read his works in the original or that there would be an explosion of doctoral dissertations on Leibniz. Nothing like that happened. Instead, what one encounters are statements about seventeenth-century philosophers that are unrelated to the topic that is being discussed but align these authors with the avant-garde. Lynn thus explains that "the mechanics of blobs ... is characterized by complex incorporations and becomings rather than by conflicts and contradictions"[337]—and then proceeds:

Leibniz's Ars combinatoria of 1666 quietly inaugurated an alternative tradition, one that does not exclude a theory of combination from discussions of order but instead makes the act of combination the primary mode of both composition and differentiation of identity. While Cartesianism is associated with the isolation and reduction of systems to their constitutive identities, Leibniz's combinatorial universe is founded on the changes in identity that take place with greater degrees of complexity and connection.

Someone who has read Leibniz's *Ars combinatoria* can only be surprised by this comparison.[338] The only similarity of Leibniz's mathematical study with blobs seems to be in the use of the term "combine" to talk about combinations of numbers and combinations of shapes in blobs. In any case, Lynn cites no works by Descartes or scholars who studied his works in order to justify his association of Cartesianism with "isolation and reduction." It is not even clear what aspects of Descartes' views he is referring to when he uses these words. However, for the revolution in architectural style that Lynn was advocating—a move from deconstructivist "confrontational" straight lines to curvy blobs—it was convenient that Deleuze's book on Leibniz identified straight lines with Descartes. Traditionally, Descartes has been the whipping boy of postmodernists, because of his association with rationality. Deleuze claimed that Descartes sought to solve problems "in rectilinear tracks, and the secret of liberty in a rectitude of the soul".[339] With Leibniz, however, "the curvature of the universe is prolonged according to three fundamental notions: the fluidity of matter, the elasticity of bodies, and the motivating spirit as a mechanism."[340] The association of straight lines with the Cartesian worldview, and ultimately Kandinsky who is described as "a Cartesian, for whom angles are firm, and for whom the point is firm" enabled Lynn to legitimize the use of curves in architecture.[341] (Note the bizarre claim that points can be *firm* or *not firm*—presumably there can be flexible, elastic, soft *points*.) The argument (if there is one) is that straight lines are bad because Deleuze says that they are Cartesian and architects should switch to curved blobs. And anyone who followed the avant-garde in those days knew that Deleuze is important and consequently switched to curved lines, for the greater glory of the avant-garde.

PARAMETRIC DESPERATIONS

Patrik Schumacher's *The Autopoiesis of Architecture* is a massive (over 1000 pages) attempt to formulate a systematic architectural theory in the post-continental-philosophy era. The book seeks to explain and promote the author's vision of Parametricism as a new hegemonic style that would dominate the profession in the future. As the book describes it, Schumacher's Parametricism is supposed to be an epochal style on par with the Renaissance, Baroque or Modernism, the new great style after Modernism.[342] It goes without saying that Schumacher sees himself as the founding father of this style. Schumacher is clearly convinced in the epochal significance of his work: towards the end of the second volume of his book he presents analyses of a number of architectural treatises that he regards as "classical": Alberti's *De re aedificatoria*, Jean Nicolas Louis Durand's *Précis des leçons d'architecture*, Le Corbusier's *Vers une architecture*, and his own *Autopoieses*.[343] It is inconceivable that someone could accuse Schumacher of false modesty.

In spite of its massive size, Schumacher's *Autopoiesis* leaves it ultimately unexplained what the motivation for this new style might be. Modernists, for instance, wanted architecture to express its time, phenomenologists wanted to make architecture express meanings and smell nicely but it is unclear what kind of ideas should motivate move to Parametricism. Instead of a clear program and aim, Schumacher's strategy seems to be to co-opt under the banner of Parametricism as many diverse contributions to the introduction of digital technology into architecture as possible. The new style, whose assumptions Schumacher seeks to articulate, has been around since the mid-1990s, he says.[344] His book is intended to make "the implicit normative self-estimations of contemporary avant-garde architecture explicit as norms."[345] The elaboration of the role of the avant-garde is one of the main themes of the book. Schumacher says that the avant-garde is the heart of the discipline, the driving force of its *autopoiesis*, the locus and the motor of the necessary development.[346] He also lists the institutions (Yale, AA School) and individuals (Eisenman, Tschumi) who belong to the avant-garde, and explains that the avant-garde has its exhibitions and magazines.[347] At the same time, mainstream professional practice serves the needs of the society.[348] Through the mainstream the avant-garde scans the maladaptation of architecture to society and the societal pressures that confront the discipline and profession as programmatic challenges that have not been anticipated.[349] The work of the avant-garde consists in finding solutions to these problems and the styles introduced by the avant-garde are design research programs.[350] (It is hard to imagine that Eisenman or Tschumi intended their work to serve such purposes.) The difference between the avant-garde and the mainstream is comparable to the difference between pure and applied science, Schumacher claims.[351] The problems that architects deal with and that the avant-garde presumably addresses belong to two "codes": utility and beauty.[352] Structural issues in his account do not belong under architecture.[353] Beauty is understood as "good, resolved form."[354] However, as we have seen earlier in this chapter, he rejects aesthetic formalism or the possibility of the attribution of aesthetic qualities to objects independently of their stylistic classification. He uses the term "formalism" not in order to refer to *aesthetic* formalism, but to the complete rejection of functional considerations, that he attributes to Eisenman and Kipnis.[355]

Once we consider what it conceals rather than what it parades, Schumacher's apparent massive self-confidence—he sees himself as the founding father of a new hegemonic style on par with the Renaissance or Baroque—reeks with profound desperation. The problem becomes obvious if we ask, on the basis of what criteria should individuals, institutions, media or exhibitions count as "avant-garde"? Innovation, Schumacher suggests, is an important criterion. However, one can be innovative in a myriad of ways, and only some of them are accepted as avant-garde. How do we know which qualities are in line with a style that is only about to be formulated, such as Parametricism? Presumably, because the avant-garde endorses these qualities. Why do some individuals count as the avant-garde and why should they decide which qualities are aligned with the new style? The only conceivable answer is that their innovations are in line with this new style, that they are about to define through their designs. In other words, parametricism is the style in which avant-garde architects design, while architects count as avant-garde if they design in the parametric style. The explanation is as good as Baron Münchhausen's claim that he managed to pull himself out of the quicksand by pulling on his own hair. Obviously, Schumacher will not admit that an individual's avant-garde status is merely a result of one's personal connections, self-promotion skills or skillful engagement in academic and professional politics. At the same time, he cannot define the type of achievement that would make an architect belong to the avant-garde without falling into circularity. The attempt to establish links with Derrida's rejection of the metaphysics of presence—presumably because evolving designs establish the meanings of previous drawings—can hardly be credible since he postulates the existence (and thus presence) of architects as authors and members of the avant-garde and the mainstream.[356] Similarly, his intention to embark "upon a consistently *anti-humanist, systematic and radically Constructivist* redescription and forward projection of architecture" may have sounded as ground-breaking and avant-garde in the 1970s.[357] Forty years later, it is painfully antiquated. In the context of his own book it is even incompatible with his discussion of the "code" of utility, since utility has to be utility for human subjects. An "anti-humanist" should not be concerned with humans' use of buildings. It thus becomes hard to avoid the unfortunate impression that when he calls his approach "anti-humanist" he is merely parroting slogans that used to qualify people as members of the avant-garde half a century ago. In other words, that the avantgardism of *Autopoiesis* belongs to a museum. However, this impression is unfair and merely illustrates a wider problem. The demise of continental philosophy has left architects and architectural theorists who want to call themselves "the avant-garde" without a source of new phrases that would qualify them as the avant-garde. Even worse, younger people (Schumacher, for instance, was born in 1961, too late to play a major role in the avant-gardes of the 1980s and the 1990s) who want to join the club cannot identify the phrases they need to use. They can only repeat the old ones. For the architectural avant-garde, the disappearance of continental philosophy introduced a serious identity crisis.

Autonomy

Let us consider Ibsen's theories about trolls once again. What makes a person a troll and not human, Ibsen says, is not being oneself. A troll, on his account, endlessly seeks enough correlations with external things and is eventually defined by these correlations. It is not clear what happens to a troll when these defining correlations disappear because the other side of correlation has vanished. (Someone might think that this happened to late twentieth-century architectural avant-garde with the demise of continental philosophy.) Ibsen does explain, however, that when a troll dies, these correlations vanish and the remaining nothing that is left is melted and recycled, into another troll. One may want to ask (and some people may actually hope!) whether architecture could be recycled in some similar way. As we have seen through this book, for the past hundred years architects and architectural academics have fought a massive and heroic struggle to reduce architecture to its correlations with its social context. By now, the struggle has been crowned with success. As a result, it is not clear that there is something architects can do that other professions cannot do better. A long time ago, architects abandoned the claim that they can resolve technical and structural issues and relinquished them to engineers. Functional problems by this time are mainly in the hands of developers. Through this book we have seen architects' systematic and consistent efforts to redirect attention from architecture's formal, visual aesthetic properties to its appropriateness to time, meanings, associations one has with it, its representational capacities and so on.[358] This tendency to reduce architecture to its social correlations has been implicit in the modernist agenda from the very beginning. Back in the 1920s Hannes Meyer argued that a building is an industrial product, made by specialists such as economists, statisticians, hygienists, climatologists, industrial engineers, standardization experts, heating engineers.[359] Consequently, all that is left for architects is to become specialists in organization—in our modern terminology, project managers. The reasoning is cogent if one accepts Meyer's assumptions and denies any relevance to aesthetic issues. Similarly, as the critics of early Chicago skyscrapers noted in the late nineteenth century, once technology becomes decisive, and ornaments are omitted, the only role that remains for an architect is that of an administrator.[360] It should not be surprising that after hundred years of such rabid correlationism many architects may start to worry. They may want to see in their profession more than an activity that ensures the compliance of building activities to codes and regulations. (And engineers can do this better too.)

It is these concerns about the autonomy of architecture that stand behind architects' and architectural theorists' interest in Object Oriented Ontology. Together with Speculative Realism, Object Oriented Ontology (or "OOO" as it is commonly referred to), can be seen as the last gasp of continental philosophical traditions. Although Speculative Realism and OOO seek to preserve philosophical links with older continental philosophical traditions, they endorse realism. By assuming that reality is not, for instance, socially or culturally constructed these approaches take a strong stance against preceding dominant streams of twentieth-century continental philosophy.[361] The philosophical style of the proponents of Speculative Realism (Quentin Meillassoux) and OOO (Graham Harman) is closer to that of analytic philosophers than to traditional continental thinkers: they present arguments, consider counterarguments, defend positions, write clearly and one can agree or disagree with what they say. Their alignment with traditional continental philosophy is based on the fact that they mainly consider and cite works of continental philosophers. (Meillassoux, for instance, actually suggests that Heidegger's sentence "[t]he appropriation appropriates man and their Being to their essential togetherness" is meaningful and that he understands its meaning.[362]) At the same time, they show little awareness of the works of analytic philosophers who have discussed similar topics and arguments as those they discuss. In other words, they lack the specialist knowledge from analytic philosophy that would help them deal with the arguments they engage with.

OOO is Harman's realist project intended to assert the autonomy of objects that exist independently of observers.[363] Since the autonomy of objects implies the autonomy of architectural works, OOO has much to promise to those architects who are interested in establishing the autonomy of architecture as a profession.[364] OOO has two main assumptions: that the ultimate stuff of the cosmos are individual entities of various different scales (not just tiny particles) and that these entities are never exhausted by any of their relations or even by the sum of all possible relations; rather, they withdraw from relations.[365] We have already seen that his argument against "undermining," the understanding of objects as sums of their parts, is not valid. This argument however has only marginal relevance for the debate about the autonomy of architecture. The fact, or our knowledge of the fact, that built buildings consist of atoms and molecules can hardly affect the autonomy of our architectural judgment. This autonomy will be, however, affected if we assume that architectural works are nothing but their correlations, if we "overmine" them as Harman put it. "Overmining" is the view that objects exist only in correlation to their social, linguistic, cultural and so on contexts. This view reduces objects to bundles of qualities or relations.[366] Typical formulations of this view assert that objects are social, cultural or linguistic constructs. As we have seen through this book, approaches based on overmining have played a huge role in debates about architecture through the twentieth century. (A good example is Kipnis's view, discussed in the third chapter of this book, that things exist only as participants in fields of linguistic reference.)

There should be no surprise that those architects who are interested in asserting the autonomy architecture are attracted by Harman's rejection of overmining.[367] The expectation is that OOO could provide a defense from the reduction of architecture to other disciplines, its social context, linguistic phenomena and so on. Harman claims that objects are autonomous in the sense that they emerge from their parts while partly *withholding* themselves from relations.[368] A table, Harman states as an example, can be conceived of as a cluster of molecules, or on the basis of our everyday relationships with it; but he advocates a third table that *"emerges* as something distinct from its own components and also *withdraws* behind all its external effects."[369] In his description, all entities tend to reside in a cryptic background rather than appear before the mind; they seldom erupt into view from the shadowy subterranean realm that supports human conscious activity.[370] Real objects, he says, cannot touch each other and their reality consists solely of being what they are, not in their impact on other things.[371] We do not interact with real objects, but with sensual objects.[372] Sensual objects exist only insofar as they are sensed by someone.[373] It can be responded that this is simply not true: a thing can have sensible properties (such as colors or warmth) without being sensed by anyone. If it reflects light with the wavelength between 625 and 740 nm, it is red regardless of whether someone sees it or not. In any case, Harman's real (withdrawn) objects are clearly separated from sensible objects and one can merely *allude* to them, but not attribute them any definite properties. Harman's response to the criticism that OOO relies on inaccessible hidden objects is precisely that one can allude to such objects indirectly or obliquely, rather than by stating their properties.[374] He says, however, preciously little about the way one can allude to a withdrawn "real" object and it is not even clear why this alluding would not count as relation. Nevertheless, the implications of the introduction of relation-independent objects for the defense of the autonomy of architecture are potentially significant. They are further strengthened by Harman's endorsement of formalism and his rejection of (what he calls) *literalism*, the view that objects can be adequately defined by relations to their contexts.[375] However, problems arise if we look at the nature of architectural qualities that OOO can vouch for. It has nothing to say about perceptible, visible, spatial properties of architectural works. At the same time, architects do not design inaccessible, withdrawn ("real" in Harman's sense) buildings. According to Harman, access to things themselves can only be indirect.[376] Real, withdrawn objects can be approached only through allusion, rather than through tangible properties.[377] In his account *allure* comes about as the result of fusion between the withdrawn real object and its sensual qualities.[378] His approach to aesthetics is then based on the claim that all of the arts produce allure.[379] Beauty is a kind of allure, whereby natural things can be also beautiful and some genuine artworks may lack beauty.[380] In his book *Art+Objects*, beauty is said to result from the tension, "the opening of a fissure" between real objects and sensible qualities.[381]

In the best possible scenario, OOO can thus safeguard architectural works from correlations insofar as they are withdrawn objects. The obvious problem is that architects do not design withdrawn invisible objects. They design buildings. Harman has little to say about the qualities of architectural works that depend on properties such as shapes, colors or their combinations. His formalism is a formalism in which such properties do not matter. This is certainly not a promising conclusion for those architects who care about the spatial, formal and visual qualities of their work. It is neither clear nor likely that architects who seek formal beauty—formalists in the traditional meaning of the term—will be willing to abandon their interests in order to seek "allure." More generally, when architects talk about "real" buildings they do not mean "withdrawn" architectural works. Harman's "allure" actually reminds of Norberg-Schulz's claim that buildings speak to us. Obviously, the response is that buildings do not speak, and the way one cannot hear what they say, it is equally impossible to identify their "allure."

The effort to seek the autonomy of architecture clearly indicates dissatisfaction with the situation in which architecture as a profession found itself after its protagonists endorsed correlationist ideologies for an entire century. It is, however, doubtful that OOO, with its anti-visual agenda, is an antidote that they are looking for. Architects—or the people who call themselves "architects" today—may now start talking about their efforts to achieve the allure of withdrawn architectural works that no one can see. Considering everything that has happened with architecture and architectural education for the past hundred years, it is, however, unlikely that a yet another theoretical redefinition of architecture as a discipline can save architecture as a profession.

Beyond Salvage?

On 28 October 312 Emperor Constantine defeated Emperor Maxentius at Saxa Rubra, seven or eight miles north-east of Rome. The next day he entered the city itself. In order to please the new ruler, the Senate decided to celebrate the event by building a monumental arch next to the Colosseum. The poor quality of the sculptural program of this structure, that was completed three years later, has attracted comments for centuries. Parts were simply taken from older buildings and re-used on the monument. Reliefs that were made for the purpose suggest poor skill of the carvers. The ineptitude in the representation of human bodies is particularly striking in comparison with Roman sculptures from the previous centuries. Writing in the eighteenth century Edward Gibbon observed that the monument

> remains a melancholy proof of the decline of the arts ... As it was not possible to find in the capital of the empire a sculptor who was capable of adorning that public monument, the Arch of Trajan ... was stripped of its most elegant figures. ... and curious antiquarians can still discover the head of Trajan on the trophies of Constantine. The new ornaments that it was necessary to introduce between the vacancies of ancient sculpture are executed in the rudest and most unskillful manner.[382]

A 1950s book by Bernard Berenson catalogues the sculptural deficiencies of the Arch.[383] Here belong undersized figures, the inaccurate size of animals, poor anatomy of human figures, huge heads out of proportion with bodies, and so on.[384] In the case of anatomically convincing parts of the sculptural program, Berenson managed to trace older Roman works from which they were copied.[385] Like Gibbon, he regarded such deficiencies as indications of decline. He also compared the sculptures from the Arch of Constantine with other sculptures of the era (the representations of contemporary Roman rulers that "look like yokels being photographed at a country fair") in which the similar trend can be observed.[386] Berenson's book was intended to oppose the views of German scholars who saw in such sculptures anticipations of the *Zeitgeist* or the Artistic Will of the Medieval era.[387] In the case of the Arch of Constantine the use of ornaments from older buildings undermines the credibility of the belief in such spiritual forces that underwrite the artistic production of entire epochs. Had they indeed acted as harbingers of a new artistic style and had their preferences been indeed determined by the spirit of the new era, the architects of the monument would not have included so many ornaments from older buildings that reflect the decidedly different taste of the previous era. It is much more convincing to agree with Berenson and attribute the re-use of these ornaments to "the feeling that nothing could be done there and then as worthy of the occasion."[388] As he put it, it is reasonable to see in the Arch "a confession of inferiority to the past, whether economic or artistic."[389]

Another way to address the dilemma is to ask whether Roman artists of the era had the training, knowledge and skills to produce work on par with that of earlier generations. If their skills and the knowledge of anatomy had been insufficient to make more accurate representations, then the spirit of the era certainly could not have *made* them choose to make anatomically less accurate representations of human bodies. If they could not have done it, then they simply had no choice. In his book, Berenson was not interested in the social context that caused the changes in art production that he described.[390] However, if we take into account political events of the preceding decades, one can hardly be surprised by the poor technical skills of the artists who worked on the Arch of Constantine. In fact, it would be surprising had Roman artistic production of the fourth century CE manifested technical skills comparable to those of the early imperial era. For a large part of the preceding century the Roman empire was heavily shaken by endless internal conflicts.[391] As the central power lost its authority, it became increasingly possible for military units to proclaim their generals into emperors, which led to a series of civil wars. It is hard to imagine that in such long-lasting circumstances a credible system of artistic education could have survived. If one looks at Berenson's criticisms of sculptures on the Arch of Constantine, they pertain to issues such as the representation of bodies and their anatomy. These are precisely the skills that would have had to be taught in order to be mastered by younger generations of artists. Even exceptionally talented sculptors cannot be expected to master alone, on their own, knowledge that generations of artists over long centuries had to discover step by step. Without systematic teaching such knowledge is lost. As T. S. Eliot observed once, a tradition cannot be inherited, it has to be acquired by hard work.[392] Certainly, the possession of skills and knowledge cannot *guarantee* creativity. Dogmatic methods of transmission are even likely to stifle it. The suppression of the transmission of skills and knowledge, however, can only guarantee incompetence.

MODERNISM, ONCE AGAIN

Without doubt, the same applies to architecture as well. Architectural works do not come about independently of the social context that enables their creation, or at least fails to prevent it. This social context need not be conceived of as an immaterial, abstract, spiritual force that comes from above. An individual architect experiences the context in thousands of interactions with his or her clients, colleagues or authorities. Mies van der Rohe or Gropius, for instance, encountered the Third Reich in numerous interactions with state officials. These state officials did not act the way they did because they were inspired by some immaterial spirit of the Nazi era. They acted in accordance with their own motivations which had to do with their ambitions, fear from higher ranking officials or their personal endorsement of Nazi ideology. Similarly, the economic pressures and constraints that imposed Modernism after World War Two were not an abstract, immaterial force that came from above. Architects who worked in those days faced them through interactions with clients, developers, government officials as well as the draftsmen and the workforce that they needed to hire. Individual motivation, often in the form of the desire to contribute to the recovery of society after the war, certainly played a huge role too. Doubtless, many architects were willing to sacrifice the ornamentation of buildings and traditional approaches to design in order to help address urgent social needs.[393] The long-term aesthetic consequences for the built environment would become obvious only some decades later.

In other words, architects' statements about their work and their advocacy of theoretical views can only be understood if we take into account their position as individuals and in relation to the social interactions, constraints and opportunities they faced. This also applies to the leading protagonists of the modernist movement in the years after the first world war. The four most prominent figures—

Frank Lloyd Wright, Mies van der Rohe, Le Corbusier or Walter Gropius—were all autodidacts. The same applies to a good number of prominent modernists of the generation born in the 1880s.* Theo van Doesburg had no architectural education at all, Antonio Sant'Elia was a drop-out and Bruno Taut's three semesters at *Baugewerbeschule* certainly cannot count as equivalent to a full architecture degree. Social circumstances prevented Wright and Mies van der Rohe from getting an academic training in architecture. Le Corbusier possibly could have found a way to get academic education but opted not to. Gropius studied architecture for two years but dropped out, probably because of his poor graphical skills.[394] (In an era when architectural education emphasized rendering and watercoloring of classical details, poor graphical skills would have been a kiss of death for a future architect.) The lack of formal education would follow them through their careers. A biographer of Mies, Elaine S. Hochman, has described Mies's "deep, pervasive, and lifelong insecurity about his intellectual qualifications."[395] When his Farnsworth project ended in a lawsuit, the client, Edith Farnsworth, complained of Mies's ignorance of high school physics.[396] In fact, Mies's formal education finished at the age of fifteen and he did not attend a high school.[397] Le Corbusier's struggle with elementary mathematics in his *Modulor* is both embarrassing and comical.[398] He shows a page of calculations that were "done by a mathematician" that could have been performed

---

* The most prominent advocates of Modernism in Europe before World War One—Peter Behrens (b. 1868), Otto Wagner (b. 1841), Adolf Loos (b. 1870) and Hendrik Petrus Berlage (b. 1856)—all had formal academic training. In the case of modernist architects who reached professional maturity after 1920, those with formal academic training (Erich Mendelsohn, Hugo Häring) never achieved prominence comparable to that of Le Corbusier, Mies or Gropius. Alvar Aalto, who is sometimes mentioned among the most prominent modernists of that generation, was actually more than ten years younger (born 1898). He is also a very anomalous figure among the modernists of his era, both because of his academic training and because of his intellectual background. In his youth he attended a tsarist-era lyceum that left him with a wide humanist education. See Schildt (ed.), *Aalto*, 16. As a result, the tone of his writing and theoretical positioning is by far more sophisticated than this is the case that of other contemporary modernists. One cannot imagine that some other modernist of the era would complain that "useless work is done by artificially seeking to mirror modern times in assignments that clearly belong to tradition in terms of content" or that "modernists make paintings which are travesties of the real art of construction or machines" or express the concern that Modernism can become "the caricature that free art becomes when it aspires to be a faithful mirror of its own era." Ibid., 63, 62, 61.

by any high school pupil.[399] At the same time, their exceptional talents are certainly beyond doubt. Works such as Mies's National Gallery in Berlin or Le Corbusier's chapel in Ronchamp are arguably major architectural masterpieces of any era. The fact that contemporary architectural academies failed to accommodate or even attract their authors when they were young certainly gives reasons to condemn the educational system of the era. In other fields too, the contemporary educational system was often more interested in the reproduction of privilege than in attracting underprivileged talents.

Since Wright was older and he lived in the USA, he did not face the same opportunities as Mies, Gropius or Le Corbusier after the end of the first world war. After 1919 their handicaps in education were massively compensated by the fact that many of their peers who did have academic training in architecture had died in the war. The opportunities that offered themselves were massive, even though they had no formal qualifications and only very meager portfolios of built work at that time. With only two years of formal architectural education Gropius became the Dean of an architecture school; in one single year, 1925, Mies came to be considered for prestigious positions in the *Kunstgewerbeschule* in Magdeburg, *Kunstakademie* in Breslau and the position of the *Stadtbaurat* in Frankfurt am Main.[400] (As mentioned, he never finished high school.) It is hard to imagine that this would have been possible had they had to compete against their peers with formal education who vanished in the tranches of the previous decade. Similar career opportunities became available to numerous young men without academic training who happened to survive the war and worked as draftsmen in architecture offices. Those who came to the forefront were those who excelled in self-promotion skills. A survey of modernist architectural theory such as Harry Francis Mallgrave's *Modern Architectural Theory* leaves one with the impression that it was primarily the use of advanced public relation techniques that the young modernists excelled in—rather than competence in the use of the latest building technologies. As Mallgrave pointed out, the ground-breaking aspect of Le Corbusier's *Toward a New Architecture* was the replacement of rational argument by a "visual catalogue specifically designed to seduce the architect."[401] The propaganda apparatus that Mies engaged in relation to the Weissenhof housing exhibition included sixty press agencies and forty correspondents.[402] Changes in personal lives also indicate ambitious positioning in relation to new opportunities. For more than a decade until 1921 Mies was carefully building his career as a traditional architect working for the Berlin upper middle class. As the new opportunities became obvious, he re-invented himself as a modernist architect. That same year he separated from his wife (whose family until then provided contacts with potential clients in Berlin bourgeoisie) and changed the last name from "Mies" to "Mies van der Rohe."[403] "Rohe" was his mother's maiden last name while "van der" was invented clearly with the intention of producing fake associations with Dutch nobility.[404] Other young modernist architects did similar things about the same time. Christian Emil Marie Küpper adopted his stepfather's name, added the aristocratically sounding "van" and became Theo van Doesburg. (It is somehow hard to take seriously the commitments to modernity of architects who parade false aristocratic titles.) In republican France Charles-Édouard Jeanneret adopted an ancestor's name "Lecorbesier" but changed it into "Le Corbusier" in order to recall names of French artists such as Charles Le Brun or André Le Nôtre.[405] Less concerned about social conventions, Wright lied about his age and presented himself two years younger than he really was.

It would be naïve to think that the theoretical positions that the protagonists of the modernist movement endorsed in the 1920s and the 1930s had nothing to do with their career prospects and efforts. Mies van der Rohe, Wright and Le Corbusier were never trained to use traditional systems of ornamentation, the classical orders or spatial composition. As a student with poor graphical skills who dropped out of architecture school, it is unlikely that Gropius ever mastered them. In order to take the advantage of the exceptional career possibilities that became available in the post-World War One era, Mies, Gropius and Le Corbusier had to argue against ornamentation and spatial composition. If they did not assert the irrelevance of the skills taught in architectural academies, they would have to admit their limited competence for the projects and commissions they aspired to get. This explains the fact, mentioned in Chapter One, that the tenets of the modernist approach to design were predominantly negative and centered on the rejection of traditional systems of ornamentation and spatial composition. These were the core elements of academic architectural training. The endorsement of flat roofs belongs to the same category. Early twentieth-century technology could not have inspired it since flat roofs leak even with technologies much more advanced than those available in those days. However, it takes more than a semester to train architecture students to design a traditional roof structure. An architect without such training will naturally seek to avoid having to design a pitched roof. (Le Corbusier and Mies did design simple roofs early in their careers, but no complex structures.) For the generation of modernists that came to the forefront in the 1920s, the only chance to realize the immense career opportunities was to argue vehemently—as they did—that the education that they did not have was obsolete in the new era. Modernism was thus not a stylistic preference. It was a path chosen because it coincided with the career and commercial interests of its protagonists. Gropius's biographer, for instance, observes that already as a student he "resisted the … prevalent philosophy of clothing new buildings in historical styles."[406] It is, however, not clear that he could do it, considering his poor graphical skills. It is in the context of this disability that we also have to understand his later tendency to inveigh in his writings against the importance of drawing skills in architecture. [407] This also explains the suppression of the teaching of perspective in the Bauhaus.[408] In his writings, lectures and interviews Mies endlessly attacked the contemporary use of the forms that he claimed belonged to the past.[409] These forms, one cannot avoid to notice, happen to be precisely those that he did not master because he lacked academic training. The same applies to Wright's persistent attacks on the Renaissance, the Renaissance style, Greek ornamentation, and so on.[410] Similarly, Le Corbusier's statement that "to send young architects to Rome is to injure them for life" is more than a mere expression of envy.[411] It is an implicit act of self-advertising intended to present the lack of opportunity as an advantage. In the context of the first half of the twentieth century, the rejection of the classical orders and spatial composition were the only reasonable strategies in the view of the career opportunities that modernist architects without academic training faced during the era. Nevertheless, had it not been for the second world war and the economic interests that became dominant in its aftermath, such views would have probably remained merely a marginal episode in the history of twentieth-century architectural debates.

MODERNISM *IS* THE CRISIS

One important problem with ignorance is that can be infectious, if it results in the suppression of education. Within a decade after World War Two the global suppression of the teaching of traditional systems

126

of ornamentation and spatial composition was almost complete. The trend was global and it is not easy to think of architectural schools that did not follow it. This could have seemed a reasonable approach to education in an era when people believed that their fantasies about the future, rather than experiences from the past, could advise them better about building for that future. By the 1970s it became impossible to hide the disastrous consequences of Modernism for the built environment. On the one hand there was the massive dissatisfaction of the general public with the works of architects. On the other, the awareness of the failure of Modernism also shook the self-confidence of architects. Postmodernist experiments with classical forms merely showed that copying and pasting is not enough in order to re-acquire what has been lost. As Joseph Brodsky put it once, culture dies for those who fail to master it.[412]

In order to understand the crisis that modernist architectural education created, it is important to understand why the simple replication of architectural ornaments from historical buildings (especially in the case of the classical tradition) does not work. The claims that classical design merely consists in the copying of historical precedents have been endlessly repeated by modernist architects and theorists.[413] In line with this misunderstanding, even a very recent author such as Schumacher asserts that "Classical architecture ... was strictly ruled by the reproduction of fixed building types, complete with proportional and ornamental system."[414] Such claims about copying or the belief that there are strictly defined rules about proportions and ornamentation merely reflect their proponents' ignorance about the complexities of classical design. There are certainly precedents and books by numerous authors such as Vignola or Palladio that provide advice about the morphology and the proportioning of ornaments. Their advices differ, and the application of the orders always depends on the architect's judgment in face of the compositional problems that arise on the specific building. Books about the orders provide advice about their *morphology* (shapes and proportions of ornaments) but say close to nothing about their *syntax*—the way they are combined. They do not explain, for instance, how to place the orders when different spatial units (such as the nave and the transept of a church) collide or how to deal with the proportions of pilasters in a staircase space, or how to relate the position of the columns on the façade to the position of internal walls. In some approaches (Palladio) the coordination of the columns on the façade with the walls inside the building implies a direct (and sometimes very complex) proportional correlation between façade composition and internal spatial composition. Resolving these details can be a formidable task even on a medium-sized building.* This is precisely why classical design can be so time-consuming and a strong reason why the architecture profession had to drop it in the post-1945 building boom.

The inclination to overlook the complexities of classical design has been fostered by arrogant dismissals that modernist historians express when they write about non-modernist architecture in the twentieth-century. It is not unreasonable to suspect that arrogance sometimes hides the lack of competence to engage with classical design. As Leon Battista Alberti put it, "it is a common vice of ignorance, to deny what one knows nothing about."[415] In the first chapter we have seen that Cohen dismissed Pope's National Gallery as "a Pantheon wrapped up in a stone sarcophagus."[416] The columns of the portico on the Pantheon are, however, Corinthian, whereas those on the National Gallery are Ionic. This has significant implications for distances between columns and consequently for the dimensions of the central circular hall behind the portico and the composition of the entire building. There seem to be, consequently, two ways to understand Cohen's statement. Either he cannot tell the difference between the Corinthian and the Ionic order, or, even worse, he thinks that the distinction is irrelevant when discussing a classical building. The former interpretation seems more likely, considering that in the same sentence he also dismissed Cass Gilbert's Supreme Court building as a "Greek Temple hybridized with a rectangular box."[417] This "temple," however, is placed on a

---

* A good example of such complexities is Palladio's treatment of the relationship between the positioning of the façade columns of Palazzo Chiericati and internal spatial composition of this building. See Mitrović, *Learning from Palladio*, 97-140. On the one hand, Palladio relied on a list of preferable room length-to-width ratios and four rules for the calculation of room heights. These ratios and rules could not be used randomly; since a series of rooms on the same floor had to have the same height, there were definite ways in which rooms with specific length-to-width-to-height ratios could be combined. On the other hand, the walls orthogonal on the facade had to align with the position of columns on the façade, with the consequence that the proportional rules for the classical orders and the disposition of columns determined the possible positions of internal walls and the proportions of rooms had to be adjusted to this requirement. At the same time, the height of rooms (as mentioned, calculated on the basis of the length-to-width ratio of the room) taken together with the thickness of the ceiling, had to be equal to the height of the column on the façade plus the entablature.

platform that clearly indicates a Roman and not a Greek precedent. It is thus fair to wonder about Cohen's elementary competence when it comes to the classical tradition. In some cases we encounter, however, not ignorance, but malicious misrepresentation of facts, quite inappropriate for historical scholarship. In his *Pioneers of Modern Design* Pevsner described how George Gilbert Scott designed British Government offices in Whitehall.[418] Scott was a Gothic revival architect and he originally wanted to design a Gothic façade. However, Lord Palmerston insisted on the Renaissance and eventually got him to do it. Pevsner reports that Scott described how he "'bought some costly books on Italian architecture and set vigorously to work' to invent an Italian façade 'beautifully got up in outline.'"[419] The account conveys the impression that classical design consists in a simple procedure of copying details from books about Italian architecture. Pevsner describes this procedure as "comedy."[420] The report actually deviously misrepresents Scott's account to the point of being fraudulent. In his *Personal and Professional Recollections* Scott indeed described how he started by buying "costly books"—but then he worked on the design the whole autumn and good part of the winter, except for six weeks when his son was ill.[421] He also travelled to Paris in order to visit important examples of classical works there, and thus recover "lost feelings for the style."[422] The design was certainly not a matter of simple copying from the books. It took almost half a year and can hardly be described as "a comedy."

This also explains why the general public today may feel to have lost communication with architects and architecture academics, the way Gregor Samsa's family could not communicate with him after he became a cockroach. One cannot go to a modernist architect and commission a Palladian building, the way Lord Palmerston commissioned it from Scott. The point is not that architects today have more commitment to Modernism than Scott had to Gothic. The point is that they cannot do it because they wouldn't know how. Tschumi, for instance, says that the aim of his Parc de la Villette project was "to prove that it was possible to construct a complex architectural organization without resorting to traditional rules of composition, hierarchy, and order."[423] It is, however, not clear that he would know how to design a complex architectural organization based on the traditional principles of composition, hierarchy and order. It is unlikely that these principles were taught in the 1960s at ETH in Zurich where he studied. Maybe he made the effort to master them on his own, but his works do not show that this was the case. It is therefore appropriate to be suspicious that the invocations of Derrida, deconstruction, groundbreaking novelties, the rejection of "tradition" are merely denials of one's own inability to do it. Talking about the USA in the 1970s, Tom Wolfe asks in his *From Bauhaus to our House*, "has there ever been another place on earth where so many people of wealth and power have paid for and put up with so much architecture they detested."[424] He observes (with apparent surprise) that great law firms of New York (and various "plutocrats, bureaucrats, board chairman, CEO's commissioners, and college presidents," he suggests) move "without a peep … into glass-box office buildings with concrete slab floors and seven-feet-ten-inch-high concrete slab ceilings and plasterboard walls and pygmy corridors."[425] There is, however, nothing to be surprised about. Money and power cannot make architects design buildings that they do not know how to design.[426] This fundamental problem could be, possibly, compared to the situation that the Gothic king of Italy Theodoric faced two centuries after Constantine. The mausoleum that Theodoric built for himself near Ravenna is covered by an imitation of a dome spanning almost 11 meters. The false dome is made of a single stone whose weight is estimated at 230 tons. The stone had to be brought to the site from Istria, hundreds of kilometers away. We do not know why an ordinary dome was not constructed. As in the case of the Arch of Constantine, some people may believe that the decision was intentional, that Theodoric wanted it so, or that the spirit of the era inspired him. But knowing the times, it is also possible that Theodoric (or his successors) had no choice. The relapse to Stonehenge-era technology may have been necessitated by the unavailability of architects who knew how to build a proper dome. If this was so, then Theodoric's predicament in matters of structure was equivalent to the one that Wolfe describes powerful American "plutocrats, bureaucrats, board chairman, CEO's commissioners, and college presidents" face in matter of aesthetics. No power or money are enough to obtain things that nobody knows how to make.

It is important to clarify that the core problem is not merely in the suppression of the classical tradition in architectural education. Because modernist buildings are often experienced as ugly additions to older urban environments it is natural to associate approaches motivated by aesthetic concerns with traditional approaches to design. The suppression of these approaches, however, is only a collateral manifestation of the anti-aesthetic ideology that dominates the profession and architecture schools. Education in architectural academies of the early twentieth century did not merely teach classical composition or neo-Gothic detailing. Classical composition and neo-Gothic detailing were its tools to teach formal aesthetic concerns in architectural design. The important point is not necessarily in teaching traditional or classical design, but in teaching aesthetic concerns. Architectural production is unlikely to avoid visual and formal ugliness if architects are taught that visual and formal-aesthetic issues do not matter. Students who go through an education in which formal-aesthetic concerns are devalued, derided and suppressed will have to unlearn everything they were taught if they want to avoid polluting the built environment with ugly buildings. This is possible, and some students do rebel, but it is also rare. By now, architectural education has been run for generations by academics inclined to deny the relevance of formal-aesthetic properties of architectural works. Students who enroll to architecture schools are taught by design professors whose design professors were taught by design professors who opposed formal-aesthetic concerns in architectural education. In the 1980s *The New York Magazine* ran an article about Eisenman. The article opens with Eisenman telling to architecture students: "You are not just going to design a building and say, 'Isn't this pretty?' ... Because that doesn't get us anywhere."[427] It is significant that a journalist writing for lay public would choose such an anti-aesthetic statement to open the article. Clearly, the statement made the point to the readers that the architect he was writing about had unexpected views about the importance of aesthetic matters. That is, in the views of the general public. Eisenman's very choice of the potentially devaluing term "pretty" clearly aimed at the dismissal of visual-aesthetic concerns. He could have chosen terms such as beautiful, nice, elegant. The statement "it does not get us anywhere" is also telling. The alternative view would be that making a building with aesthetic qualities is the highest aim an architect may seek to achieve. Arguably, there is nowhere else an architect would aspire to get.

TALKING ABOUT "ARCHITECTURE" IN THE POST-ARCHITECTURAL ERA

More than a century ago Jacob Burckhardt stated in one of his lectures that "we shall never get rid of antiquity as long as do not become barbarians again."[428] The rise of the Obfuscatory Turn in the 1970s reflected the awareness of architectural professionals and academics that this stage was reached and that there was no going back, because both architects and academics would have to retrain themselves from the beginning. Even if they did, architectural offices could not afford the return to more time-and-labor-demanding approaches design. For an architecture firm that needs to pay salaries, glass boxes and concrete bunkers are anyhow the way to go. Architecture academics who were trained under Modernism also knew that they cannot simply recover the training that most of them never received. Architectural discussions in such circumstances took the form of denials that were in line with the joint commercial interests of architects and architectural academics. Through this book, we have seen two major strategies that sought to avoid the criticism about the formal-aesthetic failure of modernist architecture and its progeny. One response was that the way buildings look, and their visual-aesthetic qualities are unimportant. Another response was that human subjects who protest against the ugliness of the newly built environments are irrelevant since it is only the views of the avant-garde that matter. All other views are to be dismissed as "populist."

Consider, as an example, the phenomenologists' claim that the problem is in modern disregard for place in opposition to space. Frampton in his article "On Reading Heidegger" complains about "our present all but total incapacity to create places."[429] "In our ubiquitous 'non-place' we congratulate ourselves regularly on our pathological capacity for abstraction," he says.[430] The cure that he proposes is "a profound consciousness of history and ... a rigorous socio-political analysis of the present, seen as a continuing fulfillment of the past."[431] In his view, "[t]he receptivity and sensitive resonance of a place ... depends first on its stability in the everyday sense and second, on the appropriateness and richness of the socio-cultural experiences it offers."[432] The problem is, however, that the profound consciousness of history, the rigor of socio-political analysis or socio-cultural experiences are perfectly useless as antidotes against formal ugliness. None of them can make people endorse a square, a street, a place, if it is surrounded by glass boxes or concrete bunkers that the people find ugly. Pallasmaa's struggle to suppress formal and visual aesthetic concerns belongs to the same strategies of denial. In the situation when visual ugliness generated by modernist architecture is a massive problem of contemporary urban environments, his protests against "aestheticisation" and claims that today's architecture purely serves "for the seduction of the eye" can only be qualified as grotesque.[433] His claim that architecture is a multisensory phenomenon—that qualities of space, matter and scale are measured equally by the eye and by the tongue—is nothing short of preposterous.[434] People simply do not go around licking buildings. It is hard to explain the wide popularity of such claims among architecture professionals and academics if one does not see in this endorsement desperate efforts to avoid and suppress any discussion of visual and formal aesthetic qualities of architecture.

It is also hard not to see similar denials in deconstructivists' theorizing as well. Consider, for instance, Beartriz Colomina's redefinition of architecture:

> ... architecture, as distinct from building, is an interpretative, critical act. It has a linguistic condition different from practical one of building. A building is interpreted when its rhetorical mechanism and principles are revealed. This analysis may be performed in a number of different ways, according to the forms of different types of discourse; among these are theory, criticism, history, and manifesto. And act of interpretation is also present in the different modes of representational discourse: drawing, writing, model making and so on. Interpretation is also integral to the art of projecting.[435]

However, *Oxford Language Dictionary* defines architecture as "the art or science of building or constructing edifices of any kind for human use"—and when it comes to the use of words such a respectable a dictionary can hardly be wrong. It is, at the same time, not clear that such an art (or science) has to be "an interpretative critical act." If architecture is defined by its "linguistic condition" and based on the analyses performed by means of theory, criticism, history and manifesto, as Colomina claims, then this means that purely visual and formal issues do not matter. Architecture and its aesthetic values are then constituted by ideas that can be associated with buildings through interpretation. On this understanding even drawings and models are architecturally relevant only on the basis of the interpretation that can be given about them. We have seen that Geoffrey Scott described this view as the "romantic fallacy." But Colomina is not merely proposing a neo-romantic redefinition of the word "architecture." The redefinition conveniently coincides with the career and commercial interests of entire generations of architects and architectural educators whose education failed to provide them with skills and abilities to engage with formal, visual-aesthetic issues. It is normal that such architects and academics would seek to supplant aesthetic concerns with stories ("interpretations") that can be told about buildings.

All this came to be massively reflected in architectural education, where tutors' anxieties and insecurities play a decisive role in the structuring of education programs. Every year, thousands of students enroll in architecture schools with the expectation to learn to practice architecture. By "architecture" they mean what the *Oxford English Dictionary* says, since this is the standard meaning of the word. This is, however, not what many of their tutors can deliver, because the education these tutors received did not provide them with material they could convey further. What teaching can be delivered by a studio tutor whose own education was based on the assumptions that engineers do structures, developers decide about planning and aesthetic issues are unimportant and arbitrary? Bamboozling students is in many cases the only reliable strategy of academic survival. A tutor with phenomenological leanings will, for instance, tell the students to go to the site, smell the air and draw the smell. A deconstructivist studio tutor will turn student's well-crafted model upside down and place it on its roof. He or she will then tell to the student to be open minded and consider alternative approaches. In both cases, the advice will include the explanation that what matters is the process and not the end result. (As if architects designed processes and not buildings.) Sometimes obfuscation fails, students realize what is going on, and protest that they are not being taught. However, since neither students nor tutors know an alternative to the present model of "architectural education," such protests change nothing. In any case, rather than condemning tutors, one should have sympathy for them. They are the original victims. Their education did not provide them with skills or knowledge that they could convey to students. When postmodernists and deconstructivists talked, in the 1980s, about post-humanism in architecture, they were making an important admission. The point is not, however, that human subjects do not exist, that they are cultural, linguistic constructs or discursive functions. The point is that architects, with the skills that they acquire in contemporary architecture schools can do little for them.

The rise of the Obfuscatory Turn in architecture thus presented a desperate response to the crisis created by the failure of Modernism. It is a strategy of a vehement, emotional denial that modernist architecture—the only kind of architecture that by the 1970s architects knew how to design and academics could teach—is visually, formally and aesthetically inferior to pre-modernist approaches to design. This connection between the Obfuscatory Turn and the failure of Modernism is further manifested by the lack of obfuscatory behavior on the side of those architects who rejected Modernism. By the late 1980s architects such as Quinlan Terry, Thomas Gordon Smith, Leon Krier, Allan Greenberg, Robert Adam, Demetri Porphyrios and others turned to the recovery of classical approaches to design. The preceding decade of post-modernist flirting with classical architecture had shown that (contrary to what modernists believed) classical detailing cannot be merely copied and pasted on the façade. In the pre-internet era, when old books were often difficult to obtain, re-discovering how classical architecture is designed turned out to be a formidable task. But the efforts of the architects and academics who chose this path have been fruitful and as a result of these efforts, classical architecture has a serious presence in the USA and the UK today, even though this work is often maligned in the media, vehemently opposed by large sections of the profession and architectural academia, and academics who want to teach it face huge difficulties when it comes to finding a job. For our discussion here this classical revival is interesting because its protagonists simply failed to engage obfuscation in their writings. Unlike the rest of the architecture profession, for the past forty years they made no significant contribution to the Obfuscatory Turn. This is hardly surprising, once we understand the Obfuscatory Turn as a particularly vehement form of the defense of Modernism. Those architects and academics who genuinely rejected Modernism had no reason to engage in its defense.

OBITUARY TO A PROFESSION.
("WHERE THINGS ARE GOING," ONCE AGAIN.)

It is hard to say something optimistic at the end of a book like this one. Possibly it is not even necessary. The book merely presents a historical phenomenon and seeks to explain it. It is the collateral factors on which this description relies—the rise of Modernism, its aesthetic failure, as well as the persistent denial of this failure by architects and architecture academics—that are disturbing and depressing. They massively affect the environment in which we live. For more than a century architects and architectural academics have sought to redefine the aims of architecture by claiming that buildings should express their time, the nature of site, meanings, the absence of presence, that it is actually the smell of buildings that matters and not the way they look—all this in desperate efforts to suppress the consideration of visual-formal aesthetic issues. Since everyone can see what is being built, the impression that such "theorizing" is merely evasion and an unconvincing denial is hard to avoid. As a result, the position and the credibility of the architectural profession and academia in modern society remains problematic. In the meantime, not only formal-aesthetic concerns have been abandoned, but also entire sectors of traditional architectural competencies, including engineering and planning, have gradually been surrendered to other professions. In our present time, after a century of frenzied relativism, it is hard to avoid the consequences. The optimistic conclusion for this book, some people may say, would be to express the hope that there is justice in this world and that a profession and academic training that contribute so little to society, and whose contributions the general public often so passionately loathes, will force itself into obsolescence and irrelevance.

The disturbing aspect of such "optimism" is not only that it is depressing, but that it is convincing. It is hard to conceive of an alternative perspective once one takes into account the powerful interests that dominate the architectural profession and academia. Nevertheless, one should differentiate here between the profession and the discipline of architecture. Things are what they are independently of the words we use in order to name them. Political circumstances or bureaucratic policies may enable individuals and groups to usurp names or impose changes in the use of words, but things do not change because we name them differently. To put it bluntly, there is architecture and then there is a type of activity that many people who call themselves "architects" call "architecture." These are not necessarily one and the same thing. The *discipline* of architecture is not necessarily tied to the *profession* that is called "architecture." Consider the question of whether purely formal-visual aesthetic properties matter in architecture. If they do not, then indeed everything that has happened for the past century with architecture was good, proper and the way it should have been. One cannot complain about the ugliness of the built environment we live in because there are no visual-formal aesthetic qualities, no ugliness or beauty, to complain about. Architecture is then nothing more than an endless series of fashions and individuals count as "architects" insofar as they follow these fashions, including (especially) fashions in verbal behavior. At the same time, it is not easy to think of anything else, in addition to architectural fashion-following, that these "architects" can do better than other professions. All they can do, from this point of view, is to follow the direction where things are going, and, from the perspective of society at large, architectural profession today is going in the direction of irrelevance and obsolescence.

The alternative view would be that all this is indeed a problem of architecture as a profession, but not of architecture as a discipline. In other words, the response would be that purely visual-formal aesthetic qualities do matter when it comes to the built environment and that architecture is the discipline that provides them. Admittedly, the judgment of large sections of the general public is that people called "architects" have been failing in this task since World War Two. Comparisons with older architecture, from this point of view, suggest that in the past architects were more competent in achieving aesthetic qualities. All this admitted, this failure is always a failure of a large number individuals who should have known better, who should have been better trained (instead, entire generations opted to undermine the educational system) and who should have shown more resistance to peer pressures. The identity of architecture as a discipline from this point of view is an aesthetic issue, independent of the failures of the profession, academia or individuals who call themselves "architects." Once they cease to care about visual-formal aesthetic qualities of the built environment, the argument goes, they cease to do architecture regardless of the words they use to describe themselves and what they are doing. The predicament of our built environment is consequently not that plenty of bad architecture is being built, but that very little real architecture is being built at all, because there are very few people who can make it. Architecture is possible in every era, but only individuals who have the necessary formal-aesthetic competence can do it. Nowadays, for reasons described in this book, such people are rare. This is not a new thing. Similar periods of massive aesthetic deprivation have happened in the past, and they can last for long periods of time, but eventually human aesthetic needs always bring architecture back. Aesthetic needs and the good taste from this point of view are hard-wired capacities of the human mind. As long there are humans, architecture (though not necessarily people who call themselves "architects") will necessarily play an important role in human society, since the need for beauty and repulsion for ugliness cannot die. To conclude, one may cite Isaac Newton: "Errors," he said, and the same certainly applies to incompetence, "belong to artists and not to art."[436]

ENDNOTES

1) The literal translation would be "Chaos, Clouds and the Tongue": "... ὀυ νομιεῖς ἤδη θεὸν οὐδενα πλὴν ... τὸ Χάος τουτὶ καὶ Νεφέλας καὶ τὴν Γλῶτταν, τρία ταυτί;" Aristophanes, *Clouds*, 421-424.

2) For a survey of such ideas see Mitrović, *Rage and Denials*.

3) In this sentence I put these two words under quotation marks in order to indicate that this is how architects and architectural academics call these approaches. I will not use quotations marks in relation to the use of these words through the rest of the book. The usage is by now standardized and this is how these approaches are called in architectural writings. One is warned, however, that similarity with what is called "Phenomenology" or "Deconstruction" in philosophy can be only superficial or even non-existent.

4) Gottfried Wilhelm Leibniz, "Antibarbarus physicus pro philosophia reali contra renovationes qualitatum scholasticarum et intelligentiarum chimaericarum," in Leibniz, *Die philosophischen Schriften*, vol. 7, 337-344, 377.

5) Scott, *The Architecture of Humanism*.

6) Ibid., 52.

7) Ibid., 96.

8) Ibid., 93, 101, 134.

9) For a systematic analysis of Alberti's views see Mitrović, *Serene Greed*, 101-146.

10) Palladio, *I quattro libri*, 1.1 says that beauty results from the relationship between parts. Guarini, *Architettura civile*, 15, says that beauty consists in the proportioned harmony between parts. For an analysis of Guarini's term *convenienza* see Mitrovič, "Guarino Guarini," 384.

In general, for aesthetic formalism in Renaissance architectural theory see Mitrović, "Aesthetic Formalism."

11) For Scott's use of the term "disinterested" see Mitrović, "Apollo's Own."

12) Ludwig Mies van der Rohe, "Bürohaus," in Neumeyer, *Kunstlose Wort*, 299. Ludwig Mies van der Rohe, "Bauen," in Neumeyer, *Kunstlose Wort*, 300-301, 300, 301. Ludwig Mies van der Rohe, "Gelöste Aufgaben. Eine Forderung an unser Bauwesen," in Neumeyer, *Kunstlose Wort*, 301-302, 302. Similarly, Ludwig Mies van der Rohe, "Über die Form in Architektur," in Neymeyer, *Kunstlose Wort*, 318. Ludwig Mies van der Rohe, "Die Voraussetzungen baukünstlerischen Schaffens. Vortrag," in Neumeyer, *Kunstlose Wort*, 362-366, 362 criticizes aesthetic attitude for superficiality. For Gropius's attacks on formalism and dismissals of aesthetic concerns see Gropius, *Internationale Architektur*, 6 and Gropius, *Die neue Architektur*, 10, 30, 54, 74.

13) See his writings collected in Neumeyer, *Das kunstlose Wort*.

14) AA.VV. "Die Erklärung von La Sarraz," in Steinmann (ed.), *Internationale Kongresse*, 28-29, 29.

15) Meyer, "Bauen," 12. Buckminster Fuller, "Universal Architecture," in Conrads (ed.), *Programs*, 128-136, 128. Behne, *Zweckbau*, 66.

16) Hermann Muthesius objected to the formalist use of historical forms of architecture, Hendrik Petrus Berlage dismissed the Renaissance use of columns and pilasters as mere decoration while Otto Wagner asserted that impractical things cannot be beautiful. Muthesius, *Stilarchitektur*, 46. Berlage, *Grundlagen*, 85. Wagner, *Moderne Architektur*, 70.

17) "Eine ästhetische Anpassung neuer Stadtteile an die historischen hat für die Entwicklung einer Stadt katastrophale Wirkung und darf in keiner Weise verlangt werden." AA.VV. "Die Feststellungen des 4. Kongresses 'Die Funktionelle Stadt,'" in Steinmann (ed.), *Internationale Kongresse*, 160-163, 163.
18) Gropius, *Apollo in Democracy*, 82, 98.
19) Wagner, *Moderne Architektur*, 50, 62. Muthesius, *Stilarchitektur*, 24.
20) Mies van der Rohe, "Bürohaus," in Neumeyer, *Kunstlose Wort*, 299-300, 299. Mies, *Conversations*, 36, 46-47, 85.
21) All citations from Gropius, *Scope*, 18, 66, 67, 67. The English version of the text on page 18 merely states "a projection of life itself." The citation here refers to the German version of the text (page 15) that says "das Leben der Zeit widerspiegeln."
22) Adolf Loos, "Die potemkinische Stadt," in Loos, *Ins Leere gesprochen*, 153-156, 155. Ludwig Mies van der Rohe, "Wohin gehen wir," in Neumeyer, *Kunstlose Wort*, 396-397, 396. Gropius, *Internationale Architektur*, 6.
23) Sant' Elia, *L'architettura*.
24) See for instance Berlage, *Gedanken*, 11 and the discussion in Singelenberg, *H. P. Berlage*, 58-59.
25) For Oud see Philip Johnson, "Mr. Oud Embroiders a Theme," and J. J. P. Oud, "Mr. Our Replies," as well as the analysis of the debate by Joan Ockman in Ockman (ed.), *Architecture Culture*, 103-106. For Stone see the account by Wolfe, *From Bauhaus*, 86-89.
26) Frank Lloyd Wright, "In the Cause of Architecture: Composition as Method in Creation," in Wright, *Collected Writings*, vol. 1, 259-262, 259.
27) Ibid., 259.
28) AA. VV. "Die Erklärung von La Sarraz," in Steinmann (ed.), *Internationale Kongresse*, 28-29, 29.

29) Sant' Elia, *Manifesto*. Gropius, *Die neue Architektur*, 20. Gropius, *Scope*, 11. Le Corbusier, *Vers une architecture*, 20, 96, 151, 153.
30) See the survey in Mitrović, *Rage and Denials*.
31) Herder, *Auch eine Philosophie*, 53.
32) For a general presentation of Lamprecht's views see Mitrović, *Rage and Denials*, 31-38.
33) See especially Lamprecht, *Einführung*. See also the analysis in Mitrović, *Rage and Denials*, 35-38.
34) Rachfahl, "Über die Theorie," 676-677.
35) Riegl, *Spätrömische Kunstindustrie*, vol. 1, 24.
36) Ibid., vol. 1, 211-212.
37) Ibid., vol. 1, 211.
38) Spengler, *Untergang*, 66.
39) Ibid., 188.
40) For a summary of some reviews see Mitrović, *Rage and Denials*, 41.
41) Pinder, *Generation*, 134. Worringer, *Formprobleme*, 116.
42) Frey, *Grundfragen*, 82.
43) Worringer, *Griechentum*, 13-14.
44) Hedicke, *Methodenlehre*, 132-135.
45) Ibid., 3, 132.
46) Ibid., 141, states that art is a product of the unity of the Spirit: "Die grundlegende Idee, der grundlegende Glaube ist dabei, daß es in jeder Zeit eine geistesgeschichtliche Einheit, ein einheitliches Wertsystem, einen einheitlichen Geist gibt und daß es letzten Endes gilt, diese Einheit, diese Wertgruppe, diesen Geist zu erkennen und darzustellen." Also, Ibid., 146: "... die gotische Kultur in ihrer Gesamtheit, ... muß auch vom Kunsthistoriker verstanden, erkannt, dargestellt werden."
47) Gombrich, *In Search*, 36.
48) Max Dvořák, "Katakombenmalereien. Die Anfänge der christlichen Kunst," in Dvořák, *Kunstgeschichte als Geistesgeschichte*, 1-40, 15. See also the analysis of Dvořák's views in Mitrović, *Rage and*

Denials, 55-58.

49) Singelenberg, *Berlage*, 58.

50) Mendelsohn, *Gesamtschaffen*, 7.

51) Taut, *Bauen*, 26.

52) Ludwig Mies van der Rohe, "Baukunst und Zeitwille" in Neumeyer, *Kunstlose Wort*, 303.

53) Ibid., 304.

54) See in particular Neumeyer, *Kunstlose Wort*, 137 and 204 for a systematic analysis of Mies's use of the term. Neumeyer observes that Mies stopped using the term after 1926, and used more general phrases "geistige Wille" and similar. Ibid., 204.

55) Mies van der Rohe, "Baukunst und Zeitwille" in Neumeyer, *Kunstlose Wort*, 303.

56) Ludwig Mies van der Rohe, "Vortrag" in Neumeyer, *Kunstlose Wort*, 311-316, 311. Similarly, Ludwig Mies van der Rohe, "Vortrag" in Neumeyer, *Kunstlose Wort*, 308-309, 308. Also, Ludwig Mies van der Rohe, "Die Voraussetzungen baukünstlerischen Schaffens," in Neumeyer, *Kunstlose Wort*, 362-366, 362.

57) Gropius, *Die neue Architektur*, 28. Gropius, *Scope*, 59. Gropius, *Apollo*, 28.

58) Pevsner, "The Architecture of Mannerism," 116.

59) All instances of Le Corbusier's use of the term *esprit* in the original French version of *Vers une architecture* that I have traced can be taken to refer to attitudes shared by (large) sets of individuals. They do not necessarily refer to a supra-individual spiritual force. His use of the term thus does not seem to have the same reference as *Geist* in the writings of contemporary German authors. Resulting interpretative dilemmas have substantially affected the translations of Le Corbusier's works. For instance, John Goodman tends to translate "esprit" as "spirit" when it is shared by groups of individuals and "mind" when Le Corbusier is talking about mental states of individuals. (Compare, for instance, translations of "esprit" in Le Corbuser *Vers une architecture*, 3 and 9 with John Goodman's translation, Le Corbusier, *Toward an architecture*, 92 and 97.) This suggests a distinction that Le Corbusier does not seem to make in *Vers une architecture*. Similarly, when Le Corbusier in his *Urbanisme* talks about the *phénomène collectif* that is instantiated in individuals he is not necessarily talking about "collective will" as Frederick Etchells translated it. (Le Corbusier, *Urbanisme*, 48 and Le Corbusier, *The City of Tomorrow*, 52) For a discussion of the methodological assumptions that generate such interpretative dilemmas, see Mitrović, *Rage and Denials*, 1-24 and Mitrović, *Materialist Philosophy*, 47-64.

60) Le Corbusier, *Vers une architecture*, 206-211 and 165-183.

61) Ibid., 172-174.

62) Ibid., 173.

63) Hitchcock, *Architecture*, 529.

64) More precisely, 147 as opposed to 24 pages. See Hitchcock, *Architecture*, 419-591. Even so, the section that is supposed to cover non-modernist works includes a number of works that would be better classified as modernist.

65) For Pope's work and design contributions to the Mall in Washington, McLeod Bedford, *Pope*.

66) Jencks, *Modern Movements*, 11.

67) Cohen, *The Future of Architecture*, 213.

68) Benevolo, *History*, vol. 1, xi.

69) Richards, *Modern Architecture*, 72.

70) Ibid., 72.

71) Cohen, *The Future of Architecture*, 102-285 for the discussion of architecture between the two world wars, 212-221.

72) Joedicke, *History*, 29, illustration 36.

73) Ibid., 114, illustration 192.

74) See illustration 142a Joedicke, *History*, 84. Also, illustration 142b, ibid., 85, for the blank wall surfaces on the Crown Hall.

75) Curtis, *Modern Architecture*, 242.

76) Cohen, *The Future of Architecture*, 212.

77) Greg Lynn, "The renewed novelty of symmetry," in Greg Lynn: *Folds, Bodies & Blobs: Collected Essays*, Place of publication not stated: La lettre volée, 2004, 63-78, 64-65.

78) Giedion, *Space, Time*, 2.

79) Ibid., 14. Later in the book he claims that "it is one of the indications of a common culture that the same problems should have arisen simultaneously and independently in both the methods of thinking and the methods of feeling." (443) This claim is then re-introduced in order to assert that "the methods of science and the methods of art came unconsciously to parallel each other about 1908." (450)

80) Ibid., 461.

81) Ibid., 22.

82) Ibid., 392.

83) Ibid., 463.

84) Ibid., 464.

85) Watkin, *Morality*, 71-121.

86) Pevsner, "The Architecture of Mannerism," *The Mint*, 1946, 116-117.

87) Pevsner, *An Outline*, 11.

88) Pevsner, *Pioneers*, 27.

89) See Rosenauer, "Max Dvořák."

90) Sedlmayr, "Quintessenz," 34. Troeltsch, *Historismus*, 37-38.

91) Adolf Loos, "Die potemkinsche Stadt" in Loos, *Ins Leere gesprochen*, 153-156, 155.

92) Le Corbusier and Pierre Jeanneret, "Analyse des éléments fondamentaux du problème de la maison minimum," in Steinmann (ed.), *Internationale Kongresse*, 60-64.

93) Le Corbusier, *Vers une architecture*, 100.

94) In the case of Mies's Lake Shore Drive, the building cost was $10.38 per square foot, which was lower than most comparable residential complexes of the day. See Schulze, *Mies*, 245.

95) Nikita Khrushchev, "Remove Shortcomings in Design, Improve Work of Architects," in Ockman, *Architecture Culture*, 185-188, 188.

96) Walter Gropius, "Is There a Science of Design," in Gropius, *Scope*, 30-43, 39.

97) For Mendelsohn see his discussion of the relativity of facts in Erich Mendelsohn, "Die internationale Übereinstimmung des neuen Beugedankes oder Dynamik und Funktion," in Mendelsohn, *Gesamtschaffen*, 22-34, 34. Giedion, *Space, Time*, 6-7. Eisenman and Krier, "'My Ideology is Better than yours,'"11. Schumacher, *Autopoiesis*, vol. 1, 54.

98) Zevi, *Language*, 17.

99) Ludwig Mies van der Rohe, "Vortrag" in Neumeyer, *Kunstlose Wort*, 323, 323. For Eisenman, see his debate with Leon Krier in Eisenman, Krier, "'My Ideology is Better than Yours,'" 15. Peter Eisenman, "The End of the Classical. The End of the Beginning, the End of the End," in Nisbett (ed.), *Theorizing*, 212-227, 216. Eisenman, "Blue Line Text," in Eisenman, *Eisenman Inside-Out*, 234-237, 234, 236.

100) Gropius, *Apollo*, 98 and *Scope*, 67. Frank Lloyd Wright, "Architect, Architecture and the Client," in Wright, *Collected Writings*, 27-38, 30. Wagner, *Modern architecture*, 118 [English translation].

101) Johnson, "Frank Lloyd Wright."

102) Nerdinger, "Bauhaus Architekten." Hochman, *Architects of Fortune.*

103) See for instance Nerdiner, "Bauhaus Architekten."

104) See Nerdinger, "Bauhaus Architekten," 156 for Gropius and 162-163 for Mies.

105) For a survey of the debate about

Le Corbusier's fascist inclinations see Brott, "The Le Corbusier Scandal."
106) Ockman, "1943," in Ockman (ed.), *Architecture Culture*, 27-28 cites Lewis Mumford's statement from 1938 that "if it is a monument, it is not modern, and if it modern it cannot be a monument" as "the accepted view" during the era.
107) Sigfried Giedion, José Luis Sert and Fernand Léger, "Nine Points on Monumentality," in Ockman (ed.), *Architecture Culture*, 29-30.
108) Palladio, *I quattro libri*, 1, Preface.
109) Scott, *Architecture*, 145.
110) Kafka, "Verwandlung." The German original actually says that he was transformed into an "Ungeziefer," a vermin, but "cockroach" seems to be a more common English translation.
111) Gropius, *Scope*, 13.
112) Mies, *Conversations*, 73.
113) Norberg-Schulz, *Intentions*, 37.
114) Ibid., 37.
115) See Mitrović, *Visuality for Architects*, for a survey of debates pertaining to New Look psychology in relation to architecture.
116) Gombrich, *Art and Illusion*. Kuhn, *Structure*. Goodman, *Languages*. Danto, *Analytical Philosophy*.
117) See especially Pylyshyn, "Is Vision Continuous with Cognition?" There exists a substantial debate about the possibility that *in some* circumstances such influences may occur, but the idea that this is *always* the case belongs to the history of the discipline. See Firestone and Scholl, "Cognition."
118) Norberg-Schulz, *Intentions*, 94.
119) Norberg-Schulz, *Intentions*, 124. Ibid, 125. Norberg-Schulz, *Architecture: Presence, Language and Place*, 173. Norberg-Schulz, *Existence, Space, Architecture,* 71. Norberg-Schulz, *Meaning in Western Architecture*, 32. Norberg-Schulz, *Genius Loci*, 66.
120) Norberg-Schulz, *Mellom jord og himmel*, 110.
121) Norberg-Schulz, *Existence, Space & Architecture*, 10.

122) Kuhn, *Structure*, 121, 134. However, in spite of such formulations, it is not clear that Kuhn really subscribed to anti-realism. See the discussion in Mitrović, "Attribution of Concepts," 325.
123) Norberg-Schulz, *Intentions*, 124.
124) Vesely, *Architecture*, ix.
125) Alberto Pérez-Gómez, "Abstraction in Modern Architecture: the Gnostic Dimension," in Pérez-Gómez, *Timely meditations*, vol. 2, 37-60, 50. Alberto Pérez-Gómez, "*Place* is not a Post-Card: The Problem of Context in Contemporary Architecture," in Pérez-Gómez, *Timely Meditations*, vol. 2, 127-141, 134.
126) Alberto Pérez-Gómez, "The Myth of Dedalus. On the Architect's *metier*," in Pérez-Gómez, *Timely Meditations*, vol. 1, 2-21, 11.
127) The Greek verb ὁράω, "I see," actually does differentiate between the active and the passive forms. Aorist active is εἶδον and passive ὤφθην; perfect active ἑόρακα or ἑώρακα and passive ἑώραμαι or ὦμμαι.
128) For a summary of satirical writings see Dieter Thomä, "Heidegger in der Satire. Das Herrchen des Seins," in Dieter Thomä (ed.), *Heidegger*, 510-513.
129) Kant, *Kritik der Urteilskraft*, 187.
130) Harman, *Quadruple Object*, 40.
131) "Inmitten des Seienden im Ganzen west eine offene Stelle. Eine Lichtung ist. Sie ist, vom Seienden her gedacht, seiender als das Seiende. Diese offene Mitte ist daher nicht vom Seienden umschlossen, sondern die lichtende Mitte selbst umkreist wie das Nichts, dass wir kaum kennen, alles Seiende." Heidegger, *Ursprung*, 56.
132) "Erde durchragt nur die Welt, Welt gründet sich nur auf die Erde, sofern die Wahrheit als der Urstreit von Lichtung und Verbergung geschieht. Aber wie geschieht Wahrheit? Wir antworten: sie geschieht in wenigen wesentlichen Weisen. Eine dieser Weisen, wie Wahrheit geschieht, ist das Werksein der Werkes. Aufstellend eine Welt und herstellend die Erde ist das Werk die Bestreitung jenes Streites, in

dem die Unverborgenheit des Seienden im Ganzen, die Wahrheit, erstritten wird." Ibid., 60.

133) Heidegger, "Bauen, Denken, Wohnen."

134) Christian Norberg-Schulz, "Heideggers tenkning om arkitektur" in Norberg-Schulz, Et sted å være, 279-287, 282. This is his Norwegian translation of his article, Norberg-Schulz, "Heidegger's Thinking about Architecture." The two versions of the article differ in various details and the Norwegian version omits the last five-and-half paragraphs from the Prospecta article. The two versions of the article need therefore to be treated as different texts. Some claims that I cite below from the Norwegian version were not originally present in the Prospecta version.

135) Ibid., 282.

136) Heidegger, Ursprung 41-42.

137) "bringer noe som er skjult i lyset," Norberg-Schulz, "Heidegger's tenkning," 280. The English version says here "it brings something into presence." Cited according to the version published in Nisbett, Theorizing, 430-439, 431.

138) Norberg-Schulz, "Heidegger's tenkning," 280.

139) Norberg-Schulz, "Concept of Dwelling," 19 Similarly, ibid., 117: "By means of the building the place gets extension and delimitation, whereby a holy precinct is formed. In other words, the meaning of the place is revealed by the building. How the building makes the destiny of the people present, is not explicit, but it is implied that this is done simultaneously with the housing of the god, which means that the fate of the people is also intimately related to the place. The visualization of the earth, finally, is taken care of by the temple's standing. It rests on the ground and towers into the air. In doing so, it gives to things their look. In general, the temple is not 'added' to the place as something foreign, but, standing there, first makes the place emerge as what it is."

140) Harman, Quadruple Object, 83. See his glorification of Heidegger in "Everything is not Connected," in Harman, Bells and Whistles, 121.

141) "Dingend verweilt das Ding die einigen Vier, Erde un Himmel, die Götlichen und die Sterblichen, in der einfalt ihres aus sich her einigen Gevierts." Cited according to Karsten Harries, "'Das Ding', 'Bauen Wohnen Denken', '... dichterisch wohnet der Mensh ...' und andere Texte aus dem Umfeld Unterwegs zum Geviert," in Thomä, ed., Heidegger, 290-302, 290.

142) Heidegger, "Bauen, Denken, Wohnen."

143) Norberg-Schulz, "Heidegger's tenkning," 282.

144) Norberg-Schulz, Concept of Dwelling, 17.

145) Ibid., 17.

146) Ibid., 17.

147) Nietzsche, Fröhliche Wissenschaft, 175-176.

148) Pallasmaa, Thinking Hand, 115.

149) Norberg-Schulz, "Heideggers tenkning," 284. Trans. Branko Mitrović.

150) Frampton, Studies, 16, 213, 222.

151) Ibid., 189.

152) Norberg-Schulz, The Concept of Dwelling, 27, caption to illustration 20.

153) Heidegger, Ursprung, 33.

154) Frampton, Studies, 239-240.

155) Ibid., 240.

156) Ibid., 240

157) Norberg-Schulz, Concept of Dwelling, 27.

158) Frampton, Studies, 286.

159) Norberg-Schulz, The Concept of Dwelling, 118.

160) Cited by Norberg-Schulz in Existence, Space and Architecture, 35.

161) Norberg-Schulz, Existence, Space and Architecture, 35.

162) Juhani Pallasmaa, "An Architecture of the Seven Senses," in Holl, Pallasmaa and Pérez-Gómez, Questions of Perception, 28-42, 30.

163) Ibid., 32. Similarly, Pallasmaa, The Eyes of the Skin, 54.

164) Norberg-Schulz, Architecture: Presence, Language and Place, 45. Italics by Norberg-Schulz.

165) Kenneth Frampton, "On Reading Heidegger," in Nisbett, *Theorizing*, 442-446, 443, 444.
166) "τὸ πέρας τοῦ περιέχοντος σώματος," Aristotle, Physics, 212a7.
167) Norberg-Schulz, *The Concept of Dwelling*, 9.
168) Ibid., 111.
169) Pallasmaa, *Thinking Hand*, 115.
170) Ibid, 19.
171) Alberti, *De re aedificatoria*, 447.
172) Pallasmaa, *Eyes of the Skin*, 22.
173) Ibid., 52.
174) Frampton, *Studies*, 1-27.
175) Ibid., 1.
176) Ibid., 8.
177) Ibid., 16.
178) Ibid., 22.
179) Ibid., 22.
180) Ibid., 23.
181) Citation according to Frampton, *Studies*, 23.
182) Ibid., 23.
183) Norberg-Schulz, "Sted og arkitektur. Trans. Branko Mitrović.
184) Ibid., 54.
185) Ibid., 54.
186) Ibid., 54.
187) Ibid., 54.
188) Ibid., 55.
189) Ibid., 55.
190) Ibid., 60.
191) Ibid., 62.
192) Ibid., 64.
193) Pallasmaa, *Embodied Image*, 26-39.
194) Ibid., 27.
195) Aristotle, *De interpretatione* according to Aristotle, *Categories, On Interpretation, Prior Analytics*, 16a4-16a8 states: "Words spoken are symbols or signs of affections or impressions of the soul; written words are the signs of words spoken. As writing, so also is speech not the same for all races of men. But the mental affections themselves, of which these words are primarily signs, are the same for the whole of mankind, as are also the objects of which those affections are representations..." Since Aristotle also insisted that the soul is the form or actuality of the body, and endorsed the view that it cannot exist without the body the "mental affections" that he talked about could not be "disembodied psychological phenomena." Aristotle, *De anima* in Aristotle, *On the Soul*, 412a6-412b1 and 414a5-414a19.
196) Aristotle, *De interpretatione*, 16a4-16a8.
197) See for instance the survey of positions in the philosophy of mind in Kim, *Philosophy of Mind*.
198) The only support that Pallasmaa offers for his claim is a second-hand citation taken from a book by a Norwegian psychologist Frode Strømnes of a claim made by two analytic philosophers, Kim Sterelny and Michael Devitt in their book *Language and Reality*. At the time Sterelny and Devitt were writing (the 1980s), the view that all thinking is verbal was indeed widespread among analytic philosophers. Even during this period, the view was rejected by a number of prominent philosophers, such as Paul Grice, Jerry Fodor, and John Searle. See Grice, "Meaning," and Grice, "Utterer's Meaning," Jerry Fodor, "Do We Think in Mentalese," in Fodor, *In Critical Condition*, 63-74 and Searle, *Intentionality*, 5. For a general history of the view that all thinking is verbal, see Losonsky, *Linguistic Turns*. Today, the view is generally rejected by analytic philosophers, see Bermúdez, *Thinking without Words*. The rare authors who insist that thoughts are language-based are careful not to formulate their claims as universal claims about all thinking. See Carruthers, *Language*, 1, 6 and Gauker, *Thinking* 1, 25.
199) Collins, *Changing Ideals*, 285.
200) Schumacher, *Autopoiesis*, vol. 1, 413.
201) In some contexts it means "distance," in accordance with the ancient Latin meaning of the term. But in about sixty contexts the word means "space" or "part of space" (for instance, the way we talk about "spaces of a house"). See the analysis in Mitrović, *Serene Greed*, 92-96.
202) Norberg-Schulz, *Meaning*,

39. He actually says: "... the Greek language does not have a single word for 'space.'" The sentence could be also understood to mean that Greek had more than one word for "space." However, his further explanation in note 29 on the same page makes it clear that he means that no word for "space" was available. He claims that "[t]he Greeks only talked about space as the 'in-between.'" He does not state the Greek word or phrase for "in-between" that he has in mind or any support for his claim.

203) Norberg-Schulz, *Existence, Space & Architecture*, 10.

204) The way he talks about χώρα in Aristotle, *Physics*, 208b33 can be understood as "space." In 209a31-209a33 he actually differentiates between the two meanings of τόπος, as "space" and "place." Like other languages (e.g. German or English) Greek did not have a word that would *exclusively* refer to space. For the history of the development of technical terms for space and place in Greek philosophy see Algra, *Concepts*, 31-71.

205) He lists τόπος, κενόν, χώρα, ἀναφής φύσις. Epicurus, "Ad Herodotum epistula prima de rerum natura," Epicurus, *Epicurea*, 58-117, 40.

206) Vesely, *Architecture*, 113.

207) Goethe, *Faust*, lines 1340-1346.

208) Jeffrey Kipnis, "Twisting the Separatrix," in Hays (ed.), *Architecture Theory*, 710-742.

209) Ibid., 716.

210) Evans, "Not to be used," 68.

211) Jacques Derrida, "Point de folie—Maintenant l'architecture," in Hays (ed.), *Architecture Theory*, 570-581, 570.

212) Ibid., 570.

213) See http://ontology.buffalo.edu/smith/varia/Derrida_Letter.htm for the 1992 petition signed by eighteen prominent analytic philosophers against Cambridge University's decision to award honorary doctorate to Derrida.

214) Rajchman, *Constructions*, 17-18.

215) Ibid., 17.

216) Ibid., 17.

217) Ibid., 18.

218) Ibid., 18.

219) Ibid., 18-19.

220) For a systematic analysis of Gombrich's views, see Mitrović, "A Defence of Light."

221) For an analysis of the debate between Gombrich and Bryson, see Mitrović, "A Defence of Light."

222) Koffka, "Zur Theori."

223) Hans Sedlmayr, "Die Quintessenz der Lehren Riegls," in Sedlmayr, *Kunst und Wahrheit*, 32-48, 46-47.

224) For summaries of debates about historical realism and anti-realism see Mitrović, *Materialist Philosophy of History*, 29-46, Murray Murphy, "Realism about the Past" and Fabrice Pataut, "Anti-Realism about the Past." The last two articles are in Tucker, *Companion*, 181-189 and 190-198.

225) As he put it: "we are confident that we have arrived at a notable degree of historical truth when those members of the historical community engaged in research on the subject in question reach a level of agreement" and "the initial plausibility of the historical way of knowing comes from the fact that so many different scholars, by applying the techniques of the discipline to the body of so-called historical evidence ... are able to achieve as broad an agreement as they actually have." Goldstein, *Historical Knowing*, 199, 200.

226) Goldstein, "History," 42.

227) For criticism see Nowell-Smith, "Constructionism."

228) Dickie, "Defining Art," 254.

229) Ibid., 256.

230) Peter Eisenman, "Vision's Unfolding. Architecture in the Age of Electronic Media," in Nesbitt (ed.), *Theorizing*, 556-561, 557. Peter Eisenman, "Introduction" in Idem, *Eisenman Inside-Out*, vii-xvi, xiv.

231) Eisenman and Krier, "My Ideology is Better than Yours," 17.

232) Peter Eisenman: "Architecture and the Problem of the Rhetorical Figure" in Nisbett (ed.), *Theorizing*, 176-181, 176.

233) Eisenman and Krier, "'My Ideology is Better than Yours,'" 11.

234) Eisenman, "Notes on Conceptual Architecture," in Eisenman, *Eisenman Inside-Out*, 11-27, 15.

235) See the analysis of this view provided by Stevens, *The Favored Circle*, 187-188. As Stevens states it, "Architectural education is intended to inculcate a certain form of habitus and provide a form of generalized embodied cultural capital, a 'cultivated' disposition." He still assumes that "young architecture graduates must know how to draw, of course they must understand building codes, the rudiments of structural analysis, the principles of construction; but right from the moment they sit down at the drawing board of their first office to the day they retire the smoothness or difficulty of their career will be mediated by their habitus acting through their cultural capital." At the same time, this cultural capital is not intellectual capital: "Architecture schools devalue intellectual capital compared to embodied cultural capital, for intellectual capital is simply not essential to achieve success."

236) Stevens, "Struggle in the Studio," 108.

237) Mark Wigley, "Deconstructivist Architecture," in Johnson and Wigley (eds), *Deconstructivist Architecture*, 10-20, 17.

238) Ibid., 17.

239) Ibid., 18.

240) Ibid., 18.

241) Ibid., 20.

242) Tschumi, "Parc de la Villette," 34.

243) Ibid., 38.

244) Peter Eisenman, "Misreading Eisenman," in Eisenman *Eisenman Inside Out*, 209-225, 218.

245) Mark Wigley, "The Translation of Architecture, the Production of Babel," in Hays (ed.), *Architecture Theory*, 661-675.

246) Peter Eisenman, "Architecture and the Problem of the Rhetorical Figure" in Nisbett (ed.), *Theorizing*, 176-181, 178, 176, 177.

247) Eisenman and Juel-Christiansen, "En samtale," 11.

248) Eisenman, "The End of the Classical," 219. Eisenman, "Misreading Peter Eisenman," 215. Vitruvius, *De architettura*, 1.1.3. Palladio, *I quttro libri*, 1.1.

249) Tschumi, *Architecture and Disjunction*, 32.

250) Eisenman, "The End of the Classical," 212. His italics.

251) Ibid., 213.

252) Ibid., 214.

253) Palladio, *I quattro libri*, 1. Preface.

254) Peter Eisenman, "Architecture as a Second Language," in Eisenman, *Eisenman Inside-Out*, 226-233, 229-230. The possibility that Alberti, in accordance with his definition of beauty, may have been concerned with the way visual elements fit together is completely suppressed. What we get is an interpretation based on Eisenman's own associations about anthropocentric and theocentric symbolism.

255) Peter Eisenman: "Post-functionalism," in Nisbett (ed.), *Theorizing*, 80-96, 82.

256) Wigley, *Architecture of Deconstruction*, 78.

257) Peter Eisenman, "Misreading Eisenman," in Eisenman, *Eisenman Inside Out*, 209-225, 222.

258) Ibid., 223.

259) Ibid., 223.

260) Liebeskind, "Fishing," 50.

261) Andersen, "Emperor's New Clothes."

262) Tschumi, *Architecture and Disjunction*, 29.

263) Aristotle *Categories*, 1b25.

264) Aristotle, *Physics*, 208a27-212a31.

265) Kant, *Kritik der reinen Vernunft*, A81.

266) Wigley, *Architecture of Deconstruction*, 27.

267) Tschumi, *Architecture and Disjunction*, 21.

268) Wigley, *Architecture of Deconstruction*, 53.

269) Benjamin, *Architectural Philosophy*, 2.

270) Ibid., 2.
271) Ibid., 3.
272) Ibid., 3.
273) Kipnis, "Nolo Contendere," 55.
274) Ibid., 55.
275) The use of the passive form ("is considered") enables Kipnis to avoid the need to identify the proponents of the bizarre and improbable view that deconstructivists presumably refute. In the next sentence he actually claims that this assumption conditions "[t]he Western critical and philosophical tradition." (Ibid., 55) No historical evidence is provided for this massive claim and it is hard to think of any.
276) "Quicquid recipitur ad modum recipientis recipitur." See for instance Bretzke, Consecrated Phrases, 116.
277) Kipnis, "Nolo Contendere," 56.
278) Ibid., 56.
279) Alberto Pérez-Gómez, "The Myth of Dedalus. On the Architect's metier," in Pérez-Gómez, Timely Meditations, vol. 1, 2-21, 11.
280) Kipnis, "Nolo Contendere," 56.
281) Eisenman, "Misreading," 214.
282) Eisenman "Architecture and the Problem of Rhetorical Figure," in Nisbett (ed.), Theorizing, 176-181, 178.
283) Eisenman and Juel-Christianesen, "En samtale," 13.
284) Eisenman, "The Representation of Doubt," in Eisenman, Eisenman Inside-Out, 144-151, 145.
285) Peter Eisenman: "Architecture and the Problem of the Rhetorical Figure," in Nisbett (ed.), Theorizing, 176-181, 176.
286) Ibid., 177.
287) Eisenman, "Misreading Peter Eisenman," 214.
288) Ibid., 214.
289) "… you can strategically insist on absence as a disruption of the system of presence, but at a certain point you have to leave the theme of absence" and he even suggested that it is necessary to compromise with the client and take use into consideration. Derrida and Eisenman, Chora L Works, 9.
290) Kipnis, "Twisting the Separatrix."
291) Ibid., 713. Note that he qualifies speaking in favor of public responsibility as "suspect."
292) Derrida, "Letter," 11.
293) Kipnis, "Twisting the Separatrix," 714-715.
294) For Derrida's dismissal of good will see Bernstein, "Conversation," 578.
295) Milosz, Native Realm, 163-164.
296) According to Eisenman's account, cited in Kipnis, "Twisting the Separatrix," 713. See also Jacques Derrida, "Why Peter Eisenman Writes Such Good Books," 116.
297) Ibsen, Peer Gynt, Act 4, lines 1197-1200
298) Richard Rorty, "Philosophy as a Kind of Writing: As Essay on Derrida," in Rorty, Consequences, 90-109.
299) See John Northam's comments on line 1199 in the fourth act of Peer Gynt. Ibsen, Peer Gynt, translated by John Northam, 184.
300) Mark Wigley, "The Translation of Architecture, the Production of Babel," in Hays (ed.), Architecture Theory, 661-675, 660.
301) Schumacher, Autopoiesis, vol.1, 121.
302) Kripke, Naming and Necessity. (The book was published in 1980, but it is a transcript of Kripke's lectures from 1970.) Putnam, "The Meaning of Meaning." Burge, "Individualism."
303) Deleuze, The Fold, 18.
304) Walton, "Categories of Art."
305) Mitrović, "Visuality and Aesthetic Formalism."
306) Zangwill, Metaphysics.
307) Harman, Immaterialism, 7-10. Harman, The Quadruple Object, 10-11.
308) Harman, Immaterialism, 7. Harman, Quadruple Object, 112, 116. Graham Harman, "The Return of Metaphysics," in Harman, Bells and Whistles, 8-30, 20.
309) Harman, Immaterialism, 41.
310) Harman, Immaterialism, 9, 27, 41. Harman, Quadruple Object, 16, 112. Harman, "The Return of Metaphysics," 20.
311) The argument is discussed, for

instance, by Ruben, "The Existence of Social Entities" and Uzquiano, "The Supreme Court." Both authors seek to show that social entities are something over and above individuals and their interactions, but they admit that the argument about replacement does not work.

312) Sykes (ed.), *Constructing*.

313) Robert Somol and Sarah Whiting, "Notes around the Doppler Effect and Other Moods of Modernism," in Sykes (ed.), *Constructing*, 190-203, 192.

314) Michael Speaks, "Design Intelligence Part 1: Introduction," in Sykes (ed.), *Constructing*, 206-215, 210.

315) Ibid, 210.

316) Roemer van Toorn, "No More Dreams? The Passion for Reality in Recent Dutch Architecture … and its Limitations," in Sykes (ed.), *Constructing*, 292-313, 293.

317) Reinhold Martin, "Critical of What? Toward a Utopian Realism," in Sykes (ed.), *Constructing*, 348-362, 348. He is summarizing with approval Baird's article "'Criticality.'"

318) Speaks, "After Theory."

319) John Rajchman, "A New Pragmatism," in Sykes (ed.), *Constructing*, 90-104.

320) Ibid., 101.

321) Ibid., 101.

322) Ibid., 102.

323) Ibid., 102.

324) Krista Sykes "Introduction. A New Pragmatism/John Rajchman," in Sykes (ed.), *Constructing*, 90-91, 90.

325) Ibid., 91.

326) Greg Lynn, "Multiplicity and Organic Bodies" in Lynn, *Folds* 33-62, 52.

327) Lynn, "Multiplicity and Organic Bodies", 39. See Sokal And Bricmont, *Fashionable Nonsense*, 110-116.

328) He cites her for the view that static characteristics are given precedence over characteristics of fluidity and summarizes her argument as the view that the inattention to fluids is linked with the proposition of "formal types" and other "symbols of universality, whose modalities of recourse to the geometric still have to be examined." Lynn, "Multiplicity", 60 (note 16). Similarly, Greg Lynn, "Body Matters" in Lynn, *Folds,* 135-156, 156 (note 14).

329) Look, "Leibniz." Jolley (ed.), *Cambridge Companion to Leibniz*.

330) Deleuze, *The Fold*, 8.

331) Sokal and Bricmont, *Fashionable Nonsense*, 154.

332) Ibid., 155.

333) Deleuze, The Fold, 18.

334) Ibid., 17.

335) Ibid., 18.

336) Ibid., 18.

337) Greg Lynn, "Blob Tectonics, or Why Tectonics is Square and Topology is Groovy" in Lynn, *Folds*, 169-182, 173.

338) Leibniz, *De arte combinatoria*.

339) Deleuze, *The Fold*, 3.

340) Ibid., 4.

341) Ibid., 14.

342) Schumacher, *Autopoiesis*, vol. 1, 253, vol. 2, 617.

343) Ibid., vol. 2, 509-605.

344) "… over the last 15 years", he says. (Ibid., vol. 2, 619) Considering that the second volume came out in 2012 and was probably written in 2011, the era of Parametricism should have started about 1996—precisely the time when computers seriously started entering architectural practices.

345) Ibid., vol. 1, xii.

346) Ibid., vol. 1, 95-96.

347) Ibid., vol. 1, 100.

348) Ibid., vol. 1, 95.

349) Ibid., vol. 1, 107.

350) Ibid., vol. 1, 277.

351) Ibid., vol. 1, 100.

352) Ibid., vol. 1, 184.

353) Ibid., vol. 1, 222.

354) Ibid., vol. 1, 221.

355) Ibid., vol. 1, 191, 205, 213.

356) Ibid., vol. 1, 343.

357) Schumacher, *Autopoiesis*, vol. 1, 56. Schumacher's italics..

358) For an explicit formulation of such concerns see in particular Gage, "Killing Simplicity."

359) Hannes Meyer, "Building," published in *Bauhaus*, Year 2, nr. 4. (1928). Cited according to Conrads

(ed.), *Programs*, 117-120, 119.

360) Mallgrave, *Modern Architectural Theory*, 280.

361) As Harman put it, "the vast majority of avant-garde thinkers since Kant have shown markedly anti-realist traits." Harman, *Quadruple Object*, 11. (Obviously, he is talking about continental philosophers.) Similarly, in "The Return to Metaphysics", *Bells and Whistles* 8-30, 11, he states that as far as he knows realism has not been defended in continental philosophy until early twenty-first century.

362) Meillassoux, *After Finitude*, 8.

363) See in particular the summary he presents in "Seventy-Six Theses on Object-Oriented Philosophy" in Harman, *Bells and Whistles*, 60-70.

364) There also exists a tendency to see in Object-Oriented Ontology merely a yet another philosophical theme from which architects could mine metaphors. See for instance Gannon, Harman, Ruy and Wiscombe: "The Object Turn," 86. See also the discussion in Norwood, "Metaphors," 115-116.

365) Harman, "Brief SR/OOO Tutorial," 7.

366) Harman, *Immaterialism*, 27. Harman, *Quadruple Object*, 11. Graham Harman, "The Four Most Typical Objections to OOO" in Harman, *Bells and Whistles*, 31-39, 35. Harman's he argument against overmining is not very good. He claims that overmining cannot explain changes in the world. The idea of the argument is that if everything were determined by its relations and here and now, and nothing hidden, there would be no reason why everything would not simply just go on being the way it already is. It can be, however, responded that relationships between objects can explain (some at least) changes that occur. If hydrochloric acid comes in contact with zinc it will dissolve the zinc. Harman, *Immaterialism*, 27. Harman, *Quadruple Object*, 12. Harman, "The Return to Metaphysics," 19. Harman, "The Four Most Typical Objections to OOO," 36.

Graham Harman, "Discovering Objects is More Important than Eliminating Them" in Harman *Bells and Whistles*, 78-99, 91.

367) Harman, *Immaterialism* 19.

369) Graham Harman: "The Third Table", 10.

370) Harman, *The Quadruple Object*, 37.

371) Ibid., 73.

372) Ibid., 74.

373) "Sensual objects would not even exist if they did not exist for me, or some other agent that expends its energy by taking them seriously." Ibid., 74. Roy Brassier's translation of Quentin Meillassoux, *After Finitude*, 2, attributes to Meillassoux the claim that *sensible* exists only as a relation. One may object that light exists even if nobody observers an illuminated object. However, later in the book Meillassoux makes it clear that he means "as-sensed" not "sensible." Ibid., 10.

374) Harman, *Art+Objects*, 30.

375) Ibid., 3.

376) Ibid., 73.

377) Harman, "Everything is not Connected," in Harman, *Bells and Whistles*, 100-127, 126.

378) Harman, *Quadruple Object*, 105. Similarly, in his Theses 62-73 in Graham Harman, "Seventy-Six Theses on Object-Oriented Philosophy," Harman, *Bells and Whistles*, 60-70, Harman calls "fusion" the tension between an object and its qualities that did not exist at its production. He also says that when tension is created between a withdrawn real object and its sensual qualities, we can speak about allure, since there is something allusive about the way the object signals to us.

379) Ibid, Thesis 66.

380) Harman, *Art+Objects*, 72-73.

381) Ibid., 24, 34.

382) Gibbon, *Decline and Fall*, vol. 1, 366-367.

383) Berenson, *The Arch of Constantine*.

384) Ibid., 25, 26, 29, 38.

385) Ibid., 34.

386) See especially his discussion of the representations of Diocletian, Massimianus Herculius, Constantius I and Galerius in the Vatican library. Ibid., 50.

387) Ibid., 32, 35.

388) Ibid., 14.

389) Ibid., 14.

390) "… we shall ignore history, whether spiritual or material, social or political." Ibid., 2.

391) See the description in Goldsworthy, *How Rome Fell*.

392) T. S. Eliot, "Tradition."

393)

394) See Rykwert, *Remembering Places*, 93-97 and 103-108 for a particularly insightful description of the enthusiasm for the new era from the perspective of an architecture student. MacCarthy, *Gropius*, 22. For Gropius' poor drafting skills see for instance MacCarthy, *Gropius*, 19, 21. She explains his withdrawal from studies by "too many interesting interruptions." Ibid., 22. However, one remains unconvinced that a student with poor drawing skills (an elementary skill for an architect, especially in those days) would have been able to graduate from the *Hochschule*.

395) Hochman, *Architects of Fortune*, 24.

396) Schulze, *Mies*, 258.

397) Ibid., 14. Schulze similarly emphasized that Mies uncommonly depended on physical models in his design process. Ibid., 284. Someone who has seen and compared different models of architectural education knows what this means: architects and students who whose training did not include descriptive geometry are notoriously handicapped in their design work because they cannot solve spatial problems using geometry. They depend on physical models instead.

398) Ibid., 229-239.

399) Le Corbusier, *Modulor* 229-239.

400) Neumeyer, *Kunstlose Wort*, 208.

401) Mallgrave, *Modern Architectural Theory*, 256.

402) Ibid., 274.

403) Schulze, *Mies*, 121.

404) As Cohen put it, Mies "embellished his name with an aristocratic flourish." Cohen, *Mies*, 28.

405) Curtis, *Le Corbusier*, 51.

406) MacCarthy, *Gropius*, 22.

407) Gropius, *Die neue Architektur*, 30, 57. Gropius, *Scope*, 53-54, 87.

408) He advertised the fact that training at the Bauhaus avoided perspective, Gropius, *Die neue Architektur*, 52.

409) Ludwig Mies van der Rohe, "Baukunst und Zeitwille!," Neumeyer, *Kunstlose Wort*, 303-306, 303. Ludwig Mies van der Rohe, "Vortrag," in Neumeyer, *Kunstlose Wort*, 308-309, 308. Ludwig Mies van der Rohe, "Vortrag," in Neumeyer, *Kunstlose Wort*, 311-316, 311.

410) See for instance, Wright, "Ausgeführte Bauten und Entwürfe von Frank Lloyd Wright," in Wright, *Collected Writings*, vol. 1, 101-115, 104, 105. Frank Lloyd Wright, "In the Cause of Architecture: Second Paper," in Wright, *Collected Writings*, vol. 1, 126-137, 136. Frank Lloyd Wright, "In the Cause of Architecture: Composition as a Method in Creation," in Wright, *Collected Writings*, vol. 1, 259-262, 259. Frank Lloyd Wright, "In the Cause of Architecture II: What Styles mean to the Architect," in Wright, *Collected Writings*, vol. 1, 263-268, 265. Frank Lloyd Wright, "The Logic of Contemporary Architecture as an Expression of this Age," in Wright, *Collected Writings*, vol. 1, 339-341, 341.

411) Le Corbusier, *Vers une architecture*, 140.

412) Brodsky, "Milan Kundera," 31.

413) Berlage, *Grundlagen*, 16 and 101, Taut, *Bauen*, 26, Gropius, *Internationale Architektur*, 5.

414) Schumacher, *Autopoiesis*, vol. 1, 342.

415) Alberti, *De re aedificatoria*, 447-449.

416) Cohen, *The Future of Architecture*, 212.

417) Ibid., 212.

418) Pevsner, *Pioneers*, 13-14.
419) Ibid., 14.
420) Ibid., 14.
421) Scott, *Recollections*, 199.
422) Ibid, 199.
423) Tschumi, "Parc de la Villette," 38.
424) Wolfe, *From Bauhaus*, 3.
425) Ibid., 5.
426) Wolfe accurately describes the suppression of non-modernist elements in architectural education imposed by modernist architects. (Ibid., 50, 54) He does not, however, analyze the implications of ignorance.
427) Taylor, "Mr In-Between," 48.
428) Cited according to Mink, Historical Understanding, 100.

429) Frampton, "On Reading Heidegger," in Nisbett (ed.), *Theorizing*, 442-446, 443.
430) Ibid., 443.
431) Ibid., 444.
432) Ibid., 444.
433) Pallasmaa, *Embodied Image*, 119.
434) Pallasmaa, *Eyes of the Skin*, 41.
435) Beatriz Colomina, "*Introduction:* On Architecture, Production and Reproduction," in Colomina and Ockman (eds), *Architectureproduction*, 7-23, 7.
436) "Attamen errores non sunt Artis sed Artificum." Newton, *Principia*, 4.

BIBLIOGRAPHY

Aalto, Alvar. See Schildt.

Alberti, Leon Battista. *De re adificatoria*. Milan: Polifilo, 1966. See also the English translation *On the Art of Building in Ten Books*. Cambridge Mass.: The MIT Press, 1988.

Algra, Keimpe. *Concepts of Space in Greek Thought*. Leiden: Brill: 1995.

Andersen, Hans Christian. "The Emperor's New Clothes." https://andersen.sdu.dk/vaerk/hersholt/TheEmperorsNewClothes_e.html. Accessed on 20 January 2021.

Aquinas, Thomas. *Summa theologiae angelici doctoris Sancti Thomae Aquinatis*. http://www.thelatinlibrary.com/aquinas. Accessed on 28 February 2021.

Aristophanes. *Clouds. Wasps. Peace*. Cambridge, Mass.: Harvard University Press, 1998.

Aristotle. *De interpretatione*. According to Aristotle, *Categories, On Interpretation, Prior Analytics*, Cambridge, Mass.: Harvard University Press, 1996.

-----. *Physics*. Cambridge, Mass.: Harvard University Press, 1996. (2 vols).

-----. *De anima*. According to Aristotle, *On the Soul, Parva naturalia, On Breath*. Cambridge, Mass.: Harvard University Press, 1995.

Banham, Reynar. *Theory and Design in the First Machine Age*. London: The Architectural Press, 1962.

Behne, Adolf. *Der moderne Zweckbau*. Berlin: Ulstein, 1964.

Benevolo, Leonardo. *History of Modern Architecture*. London: Routledge & Kegan Paul, 1971. (2 vols).

Benjamin, Andrew. *The Plural Event: Descartes, Hegel, Heidegger*. London: Routledge, 1993.

-----. *Architectural Philosophy*. London: The Athlone Press, 2000.

Berenson, Bernard. *The Arch of Constantine or the Decline of Form*. London: Chapman & Hall, 1954.

Berlage, Hendrik Petrus. *Grundlagen & Entwicklung der Architektur*. Berlin: Julius Bard, 1908.

Bermúdez, José Luis. *Thinking without Words*. Oxford: Oxford University Press, 2003.

Bernstein, Richard. "The Conversation That Never Happened." *The Review of Metaphysics*. 61 (2008): 577-603, 578.

Bretzke, James. *Consecrated Phrases: A Latin Theological Dictionary*. Collegeville: The Liturgical Press, 2003.

Brodsky, Joseph. "Why Milan Kundera is Wrong about Dostoyevsky." *New York Times*. February 17, 1985, 31.

Brott, Simone. "The Le Corbusier Scandal, or was Le Corbusier a Fascist?" *Fascism*. 6 (2017): 196-227.

Burge, Tyler. "Individualism and the Mental." *Midwest Studies in Philosophy*. 4 (1979): 73-122.

Carruthers, Peter. *Language, Thought and Consciousness*. Cambridge: Cambridge University Press, 1996.

Collins, Peter. *Changing Ideals in Modern Architecture*. London: Faber and Faber, 1965.

Colomina, Beatriz and Joan Ockman (eds). *Architectureproduction*. New York: Princeton Architectural Press, 1988.

Conrads, Ulrich (ed.). *Programs and Manifestos on 20th-Century Architecture*. Cambridge, Mass.: The MIT Press, 1971.

Curtis, William. *Modern Architecture since 1900*. Oxford: Phaidon, 1987.

-----. *Le Corbusier: Ideas and Forms.* London: Phaidon, 1999.

Danto, Arthur. *The Analytical Philosophy of History.* Cambridge: Cambridge University Press, 1965.

Deleuze, Gilles. *The Fold: Leibniz and the Baroque.* Minneapolis: University of Minnesota Press, 1993,

Derrida, Jacques and Hilary Henel. "A Letter to Peter Eisenman." *Assemblage.* 12 (1990): 6-13.

Derrida, Jacques. "Why Peter Eisenman Writes Such Good Books." *Architecture and Urbanism.* 8 (1988): 113-124.

Dickie, George. "Defining Art." *American Philosophical Quarterly.* 6 (1969): 253-256.

Dvořák, Max. *Kunstgeschichte als Geistesgeschichte.* Munich: Piper, 1924.

Eisenman, Peter. *Eisenman Inside Out: Selected Writings 1963-1988.* Yale University Press: New Haven, 2004.

Peter Eisenman and Carsten Juel-Christiansen. "Peter Eisenman. En samtale ved Carsten Juel Christiansen." *Skala,* 12 (1987): 9-13.

Eisenman, Peter and Leon Krier. "My Ideology is Better than Yours." *Architectural Design.* 59 (1994): 7-18.

Eliot, T. S. "Tradition and the Individual Talent." https://people.unica.it/fiorenzoiuliano/files/2017/05/tradition-and-the-individual-talent.pdf. Accessed on 16 September 2020.

Epicurus. *Epicurea.* Milan: Bompiani, 2002.

Evans, Robin. "Not to be Used for Wrapping Purposes." *AA Files.* 10 (1985): 68-78.

Firestone, Chaz and Brian Scholl. "Cognition does not Affect Perception: Evaluating the Evidence for 'Top-Down' Effects." *Behavioral and Brain Sciences.* 39 (2016): 1-77.

Fodor, Jerry. *In Critical Condition: Polemical Essays on Cognitive Science and the Philosophy of Mind.* Cambridge, Mass.: MIT Press, 1998.

Frampton, Kenneth. *Studies in Tectonic Culture: The Poetics of Construction in Nineteenth and Twentieth Century Architecture.* Cambridge, Mass.: The MIT Press, 1995.

Frey, Dagobert. *Kunstwissenschaftliche Grundfragen: Prolegomena zu einer Kunstphilosophie.* Darmstadt: Wissenschaftliche Buchgeselschaft, 1992.

Gage, Mark. "Killing Simplicity: Object Oriented Philosophy in Architecture." *Log.* 33 (2015): 95-106.

Gannon, Todd, Graham Harman, David Ruy and Tom Wiscombe. "The Object Turn: A Conversation." *Log.* 33 (2015): 73-94.

Gauker, Christopher. *Thinking Out Loud.* Princeton: Princeton University Press, 1994.

Gibbon, Edward. *The Decline and Fall of the Roman Empire.* New York: The Modern Library. The year of publication not stated. (3 vols).

Giedion, Siegfried. *Space Time and Architecture. The Growth of a New Tradition.* Cambridge, Mass.: Harvard University Press, 2008.

Goethe, Johann Wolfgang. *Faust: Erster und zweiter Teil.* Munich: DTV, 1977.

Goldstein, Leon. *Historical Knowing.* Austin: University of Texas Press, 1976.

-----. "History and the Primacy of Knowing." *History and Theory.* 16 (1977): 29-52.

Goldsworthy, Adrian. *How Rome Fell.* New Haven: Yale University Press, 2009.

Gombrich, Ernst. *Art and Illusion.* London: Pantheon Books, 1960.

-----. *In Search for Cultural History.* Oxford: Oxford University Press, 1969.

Goodman, Nelson. *Languages of Art: An Approach to a Theory of Symbols.* Indianapolis: Bobbs-Merrill, 1968.

Gössel, Peter and Gabriele Leuthäuser. *Architektur des 20. Jahrhunderts.* Cologne: Benedikt Taschenverlag, 1990.

Gropius, Walter. *Programm des staatlichen Bauhauses in Weimar.* Weimar: Bauhaus, 1919.

-----. *Internationale Architektur.* Munich: Albert Langen Verlag, 1925.

-----. *Die neue Architektur und das Bauhaus.* Mainz: Florian Kupferberg, 1967. (Originally published in English but based on a German original manuscript).

-----. *Scope of Total Architecture.* New York: Harper & Broth, 1955. Cited according to the 1962 edition, New York: Collier Books. See also the German edition: *Architektur: Wege zu einer optischen Kultur.* Frankfurt am Main: Fischer, 1956.

-----. *Apollo in Democracy: The Cultural Obligation of the Architect.* New York: McGrow-Hill, 1968.

Grice, Paul. "Meaning." *Philosophical Review.* 66 (1957): 378-388.

-----. "Utterer's Meaning and Intention." *Philosophical Review.* 78 (1969): 147-177.

Guarini, Guarino. *Architettura civile.* Milan: Polifilo, 1968.

Holl, Steven, Juhani Pallasmaa and Alberto Pérez-Gómez. *Questions of Perception: Phenomenology of Architecture.* San Francisco: William Stout, 2006.

Harman, Graham. *The Quadruple Object.* Winchester: Zero Books, 2011.

-----. "The Third Table." In *Documenta: 100 Notes-100 Thoughts,* edited by Katrin Sauerländer, 4-16. Place of publication not stated: 2012.

-----. *Bells and Whistles.* Winchester: Zero Books, 2013.

-----. *Immaterialism: Objects and Social Theory.* Cambridge: Polity, 2016.

-----. *Art+Objects.* Cambridge: Polity, 2020.

Hays, Michael (ed.). *Oppositions Reader.* New York: Princeton Architectural Press, 1998.

----- (ed.). *Architecture Theory since 1968.* Cambridge, Mass.: The MIT Press, 1998.

Hedicke, Robert. *Methodenlehre der Kunstgeschichte: Ein Handbuch für Studierende.* Strassburg: Heitz, 1924.

Heidegger, Martin. *Der Ursprung des Kunstwerkes.* Stuttgart: Philipp Reclam, 1960.

-----. "Bauen, Denken, Wohnen." https://docplayer.org/24892585-Martin-heidegger-bauen-wohnen-denken.html. Accessed on 21 February 2021.

Herder, Johann Gottfried. *Auch eine Philosophie der Geschichte zur Bildung der Menschheit.* Stuttgart: Reclam, 1990.

Hitchcock, Henry-Russell. *Architecture: Nineteenth and Twentieth Centuries.* Hew Haven: Yale University Press, 1987.

Hochman, Elaine. *Architects of Fortune.* New York: Fromm International Publishing Corporation, 1990.

Ibsen, Henrik. *Peer Gynt: A Dramatic Poem.* English translation and comments by John Northam. Oslo: Scandinavian University Press, 1995.

Jencks, Charles. *Modern Movements in Architecture.* Harmondsworth: Penguin Books, 1973.

Joedicke, Jürgen. *A History of Modern Architecture.* London: Architectural Press, 1959.

Johnson, Donald Leslie. "Frank Lloyd Wright in Moscow: June 1937." *Journal of the Society of Architectural Historians.* 46 (1987): 65-79.

Johnson, Philip and Mark Wigley (eds). *Deconstructivist Architecture.* New York: Museum of Modern Art, 1988.

Jolley, Nicholas (ed.). *The Cambridge Companion to Leibniz*. Cambridge: Cambridge University Press, 1995.

Kafka, Franz. "Verwandlung." http://www.digbib.org/Franz_Kafka_1883/Die_Verwandlung_.pdf. Accessed on 20 February 2021.

Kant, Immanuel. *Kritik der reinen Vernunft*. Leipzig: Reclam, 1979.

-----. *Kritik der Urteilskraft*. Stuttgart: Philip Reclam, 1963.

Kim, Jaegwon. *Philosophy of Mind*. Boulder: Westerview Press, 2011.

Kipnis, Jeffrey. "Nolo Contendere." *Assemblage*. 11 (1990): 54-57.

Koffka, Kurt. "Zur Theorie der Erlebnis-Wahrnehmung." *Annalen der Philosophie*. 3 (1923): 375-399.

Kripke, Saul. *Naming and Necessity*. Cambridge, Mass.: Harvard University Press, 1980.

Kuhn, Thomas. *Structure of Scientific Revolutions*. Chicago: University of Chicago Press, 1962.

Lamprecht Karl. *Einführung in das historische Denken*. Leipzig: Voigtländer, 1912.

Le Corbusier. *Vers une architecture*. Paris: Les Editions G. Crès, 1924. English translation by John Goodman: Le Corbusier: *Toward an Architecture*. Los Angeles: The Getty Research Institute, 2007.

-----. *Urbanisme*. Paris: Les Editions G. Cres, 1925. English translation by Frederick Etchells: *The City of Tomorrow*. London: The Architectural Press, 1987.

-----. *Le Corbusier - Œuvre complète*. Volume 1: 1910-1929. Edited by Willy Boesiger and Oscar Stonorov. Basle: Birkhäuser, 2015.

-----. *Modulor*. London: Faber and Faber, 1961.

Leibniz, Gottfried Wilhelm. *De arte combinatoria*. Leipzig: Johannes Simon Fickius and Johannes Polycarp Sauboldus, 1666. https://ia800906.us.archive.org/14/items/ita-bnc-mag-00000844-001/ita-bnc-mag-00000844-001.pdf. Accessed on 9 March 2020.

-----. *Die philosophischen Schriften*. Hildesheim: Georg Olms Verlagsbuchhandlung, 1961.

Look, Brandon C. "Gottfried Wilhelm Leibniz." In *The Stanford Encyclopedia of Philosophy* edited by Edward N. Zalta. https://plato.stanford.edu/archives/spr2020/entries/leibniz/. Accessed on 20 February 2021.

Loos, Adolf. *Ins Leere gesprochen 1897-1900. Trotzdem 1900-1930*. Vienna: Herold, 1962.

Losonsky, Michael. *Linguistic Turns in Modern Philosophy*. Cambridge: Cambridge University Press, 2006.

Lynn, Greg. *Animate Form*. New York: Princeton Architectural Press, 1999.

-----. *Folds, Bodies & Blobs: Collected Essays*. Place of publication not stated: La lettre volée, 2004.

Lynn, Greg (ed.). *Folding in Architecture: Revised Edition*. Chichester: Wiley-Academy, 2004.

MacCarthy, Fiona. *Walter Gropius. Visionary Founder of the Bauhaus*. London: Faber & Faber, 2019.

Mallgrave, Harry Francis. *Modern Architectural Theory: A Historical Survey 1673-1968*. Cambridge: Cambridge University Press, 2006.

McLoad Bedford, Steven. *John Russell Pope: Architect of Empire*. New York: Rizzoli, 1998.

Meinecke, Friedrich. *Die Entstehung des Historismus*. Munich: Leibniz Verlag, 1946.

Mendelsohn, Erich. *Das Gesamtschaffen des Architekten: Skizzen-Entwürfe-Bauten*. Berlin: Rudolf Mosse Buchverlag, 1930.

Meyer, Hannes. "Bauen." *Bauhaus* 2 (1928): number 4, 12-13.

Mies van der Rohe, Ludwig. *Conversations with Mies van der Rohe*. New York: Princeton Architectural Press, 2006.

Milosz, Czeslaw. *Native Realm*. New York: Farrar, Straus and Giroux, 2002.

Mink, Louis. *Historical Understanding*. Ithaca: Cornell University Press, 1987.

Mitrović, Branko. "Apollo's Own: Geoffrey Scott and the Lost Pleasures of Architectural History." *Journal of Architectural Education*. 54 (2000): 95-103.

-----. "Aesthetic Formalism in Renaissance Architectural Theory." *Zeitschrift für Kunstgeschichte*. 66 (2003): 321-339.

-----. *Learning from Palladio*. New York: Norton, 2004.

-----. *Serene Greed of the Eye: Leon Battista Alberti and the Philosophical Foundations of Renaissance Architectural Theory*. Berlin: Deutscher Kunstverlag, 2005.

-----. "Attribution of Concepts and Problems with Anachronism." *History and Theory*. 50 (2011): 303-327.

-----. *Rage and Denials: Collectivist Philosophy, Politics and Art Historiography 1890-1947*. University Park: Penn State University Press, 2015.

-----. "Visuality and Aesthetic Formalism." *British Journal of Aesthetics*. 58 (2018): 147-163.

-----. "Guarino Guarini's Architectural Theory and Counter-Reformation Aristotelianism: Visuality and Aesthetics in *Architettura civile* and *Placita philosophica*." *I Tatti Studies*. 23 (2020): 375-396.

-----. *Materialist Philosophy of History: A Realist Antidote to Postmodernism*. Lanham: Lexington, 2020.

Muthesius, Hermann. *Stilarchitektur und Baukunst*. Mühheim-Ruhr: Schimmelpfeng, 1902.

Nerdinger, Winfred. "Bauhaus-Architekten im 'Dritten Reich.'" In *Bauhaus-Moderne im Nationalsozialismus*, edited by Winfred Nerdinger, 113-141. Munich: Prestel, 1993.

Neumeyer, Fritz. *Mies van der Rohe: Das kunstlose Wort*. Berlin: Siedler 1986.

Newton, Isaac. *Philosophiae naturalis principia mathematica*. London: Royal Society, 1687.

Nietzsche, Friedrich. *Die fröhliche Wissenschaft*. Leipzig: E. W. Fritzsch, 1887.

Nisbett, Kate (ed.). *Theorizing a New Agenda for Architecture. An Anthology of Architectural Theory 1965-1995*. New York: Princeton Architectural Press, 1996.

Norberg-Schulz, Christian. *Intentions in Architecture*. Oslo: Universitetsforlaget, 1966.

-----. *Existence, Space & Architecture*. London: Studio Vista, 1971.

-----. *Meaning in Western Architecture*. New York: Rizzoli 1980.

-----. *Genius Loci: Towards a Phenomenology of Architecture*. New York: Rizzoli, 1980.

-----. "Heidegger's Thinking about Architecture." *Prospecta*. 20 (1983): 61-68. Cited according to the version published in Nisbett (ed.): *Theorizing*, 430-439.

-----. *The Concept of Dwelling: On the Way to Figurative Architecture*. New York: Rizzoli 1985.

-----. *Et sted å være: Essays og artikler*. Oslo: Gyldendal, 1986.

-----. *Mellom jord og himmel: En bok om steder og hus*. Oslo: Pax Forlag, 1992.

-----. *Architecture: Presence, Language and Place*. Milan: Skira, 2000.

Norwood, Bryan. "Metaphors for Nothing." *Log*. 33 (2015): 107-119.

Nowell-Smith, Patrick Horace. "The Constructionism Theory of History." *History and Theory*. 16 (1977): 1-28.

Ockman, Joan (ed.). *Architecture Culture 1943-1968*. New York: Rizzoli, 1993.

Palladio, Andrea. *I quattro libri dell'architettura*. Pordenone: Studio Tesi, 1992.

Pallasmaa, Juhani. *The Eyes of the Skin: Architecture and the Senses*. Chichester: Wiley, 2005.

-----. *The Thinking Hand: Existential and Embodied Wisdom in Architecture*. Chichester: Wiley, 2009.

-----. *The Embodied Image: Imagination and Imagery in Architecture*. Chichester: Wiley, 2011.

Pérez-Gómez, Alberto. *Attunement: Architectural Meaning after the Crisis of Modern Science*. Cambridge, Mass: The MIT Press, 2016.

-----. *Timely Meditations: Selected Essays on Architecture*. Montreal: Right Angle International, 2016. (2 vols).

Pevsner, Nikolaus. "The Architecture of Mannerism." In *The Mint: A Miscellany of Literature, Art and Criticism*, edited by Geoffrey Grigson, 116-138. London: Routledge and Sons, 1946.

-----. *An Outline of European Architecture*. London: Thames & Hudson, 2009.

-----. *Pioneers of Modern Design*. New Haven: Yale University Press, 2005.

Pinder, Wilhelm. *Das Problem der Generation in der Kunstgeschichte Europas*. Berlin: Frankfurter Verlags-Anstalt, 1926.

Putnam, Hilary. "The Meaning of Meaning." *Minnesota Studies in the Philosophy of Science*. 7 (1979): 131-193.

Pylyshyn, Zenon. "Is Vision Continuous with Cognition? The Case for Cognitive Impenetrability of Visual Perception." *Behavioural and Brain Sciences*. 22 (1999): 341-423.

Rachfahl, Felix. "Über die Theorie einer kollektivistischen Geschichtswissenschaft." *Jahrbücher für Nationalökonomie und Statistik*. 68 (1897): 659-689.

Rajchman, John. *Constructions*. Cambridge, Mass.: The MIT Press, 1998.

Riegl, Alois. *Spätrömische Kunstindustrie nach den Funden in Österreich-Ungarn*. Vienna: K-K Hof-und-Staatsdruckerei, 1901. (2 vols).

Rorty, Richard. *Consequences of Pragmatism*. Minneapolis: University of Minnesota Press, 1982.

Ruben, David-Hillel. "The Existence of Social Entities." *The Philosophical Quarterly*. 32 (1982): 295-310.

Sant'Elia, Antonio. *L'architettura futurista: Manifesto*. Milan: Direzione del movimento futurista, 1914.

Schildt, Göran (ed.). *Alvar Aalto in his Words*. New York: Rizzoli 1997.

Schulze, Franz. *Mies van der Rohe: A Critical Biography*. Chicago: The University of Chicago Press, 1985.

Schumacher, Patrik. *The Autopoiesis of Architecture: A New Framework for Architecture*. Chichester: John Wiley & Sons, 2011.

Scott, Geoffrey. *The Architecture of Humanism*. New York: W.W. Norton & Company, 1974.

Scott, George Gilbert. *Personal and Professional Recollections*. London: Sampson Low, Marston, Searle and Rivington, 1879.

Searle, John. *Intentionality*. Cambridge: Cambridge University Press, 1983.

Sedlmayr, Hans. *Kunst und Wahrheit*. Mittenwald: Mäander, 1978.

Singelenberg, Pieter. *H. P. Berlage Idea and Style The Quest for Modern Architecture*. Utrecht: Haentjens Dekker & Gumbert, 1972.

Speaks, Michael. "After Theory." *Architectural Record*. 193 (2005): 72-75.

Spengler, Oswald. *Der Untergang des Abendlandes. Umrisse einer Morphologie der Welgeschichte*. Munich: DTV 2003.

Steinmann, Martin (ed.). *Internationale Kongresse für Neues Bauen. Congrès Internationaux d'Architecture Moderne. Dokumente 1928-1939*. Basle: Birkhäuser, 1979.

Sterelny, Kim and Michael Devitt. *Language and Reality*. Cambridge, Mass.: The MIT Press, 1987.

Stevens, Garry. "Struggle in the Studio: A Bourdivin Look at Architectural Pedagogy." *Journal of Architectural Education*. 49 (1995): 105-122.

-----. *The Favored Circle*. Cambridge, Mass.: The MIT Press, 1998.

Stoljar, Daniel. "Physicalism." In *The Stanford Encyclopedia of Philosophy* edited by Edward N. Zalta. https://plato.stanford.edu/entries/physicalism/. Accessed on 27 December 2018.

Sykes, Kristina (ed.). *Constructing a New Agenda: Architectural Theory 1993-2009*. New York: Princeton Architectural Press, 2010.

Taut, Bruno. *Bauen Der neue Wohnbau*. Leipzig: Klinkhardt & Biermann, the year of publication not stated.

Taylor, John. "Mr In-Between. Deconstructing with Peter Eisenman." *New York Magazine*. October 17, 1988, 46-52.

Thomä, Dieter (ed.). *Heidegger Handbuch Leben-Werk-Wirkung*. Stuttgart: Metzler, 2003.

Troeltsch, Ernst. *Der Historismus und seine Probleme: Das logische Problem der Geschichtsphilosophie*. Tübingen: J. C. B. Mohr, 1922.

-----. *Lesebuch: Ausgewählte Texte*. Tübingen: Mohr Siebeck, 2003.

Tschumi, Bernard. *Architecture and Disjunction*. Cambridge Mass.: The MIT Press, 2001.

Tucker, Aviezer (ed.). *A Companion to the Philosophy of History and Historiography*. Chichester: John Wiley & Sons, 2011.

Uzquiano, Gabriel. "The Supreme Court and the Supreme Court Justices: A Metaphysical Puzzle." *Nous*, 38 (2004): 135-153.

Vesely, Dalibor. *Architecture in the Age of Divided Representation*. Cambridge, Mass.: The MIT Press, 2004.

Vitruvius, Marcus Pollio. *De architectura libri decem*. Cambridge, Mass.: Harvard University Press, 1973. (2 vols).

Wagner, Otto. *Moderne Architektur*. Vienna: Anton Schroll, 1902. See also the English translation with Introduction by Harry Francis Mallgrave, *Modern Architecture*, Santa Monica: The Getty Center for the History of Art and the Humanities, 1988.

Walton, Kendall. "Categories of Art." *Philosophical Review*. 79 (1970): 334-367.

Wigley, Mark. *The Architecture of Deconstruction: Derrida's Haunt*. Cambridge, Mass.: The MIT Press, 1995.

Wolfe, Tom. *From Bauhaus to our House*. London: Abacus, 1983.

Worringer, Wilhelm. *Formprobleme der Gotik*. Munich: R. Piper, 1920.

-----. *Griechentum und Gotik*. Munich: R. Piper & Co. Verlag, 1928.

Wright, Frank Lloyd. *Collected Writings*. New York: Rizzoli 1992. (3 vols).

Zangwill, Nick. *Metaphysics of Beauty*. Ithaca: Cornell University Press, 2001.

Zevi, Bruno. *The Modern Language of Architecture*. New York: Da Capo Press, 1994.

INDEX

Aalto, Alvar 123
Adam, Robert 135
Alberti, Leon Battista 17, 61, 67, 85, 96, 113, 128
Andersen, Hans Christian 90
Apollo 48
Aristophanes 9
Aristotle 67, 68, 90
Augustine of Hippo 25
Bauhaus 18, 28, 41
Behne, Adolf 18
Behrens, Peter 39, 63, 123
Benevolo, Leonardo 31
Benjamin, Andrew 90, 93
Berenson, Bernard 120, 121
Berlage, Hendrik Petrus 18, 27, 39, 123
Bloomfield, Reginald 33
Bonaparte, Napoleon 26
Brasini, Armando 29, 32
Bricmont, Jean 15, 109
Brodsky, Joseph 127
Bryson, Norman 78
Bulgakov, Mikhail Afanasyevich 71, 100, 101
Burckhardt, Jacob 131
Cass, Gilbert 128
CIAM 18, 22, 38, 41
Cohen, Jean-Louis 31, 32, 33, 128, 129
Collins, Peter 67
Colomina, Beatriz 133
Constantine, Flavius Valerius 120, 130
Curtis, Willam 33
Danto, Arthur 47, 79
Deconstruction 13, 71-100,
Deleuze, Jules 71, 72, 73, 75, 76, 102, 104, 106, 109-112
Derrida, Jacques 71-74, 91, 99, 100, 102-104, 114, 129
Descartes 91, 112
Dickie, George 79
Doesburg, Theo 123, 125
Dostoevsky, Fyodor Mikhailovich 71, 100, 101
Duchamp, Marcel 80
Durand, Jean Nicolas Luis 113
Dvořák, Max 27, 36
Einstein, Albert 63

Eisenman, Peter 40, 41, 73, 80, 82-87, 97, 98, 99, 100, 103, 106, 107, 113, 114, 131
Eliot, Thomas Stearns 122
Epicurus 68, 91
Euclid 68
Farnsworth, Edith 123
Flagg, Ernest 32
Foucault, Michel 71-73, 102
Frampton, Kenneth 57, 58, 60, 62, 64, 132
Frey, Dagobert 26
Fuller, Buckminster 18,
Gadamer, Hans-Georg 99
Gibbon, Edward 120
Giedeon , Siegfried 34-37, 40
Goethe, Johann Wolfgang 71, 100, 101
Goldstein, Leon 78, 81, 83
Gombrich, Ernst 27, 47, 77
Goodman, Nelson 47
Grass, Günter 51
Greenberg, Allan 135
Gropius, Walter 10, 17, 19, 20, 23, 28, 35, 37, 40, 41, 45, 103, 122-126
Guarini, Guarino 17, 96
Häring, Hugo 123
Harman, Graham 51, 53, 105, 115-119
Harries, Karstens 53
Hays, Michael 106, 107
Hedicke, Robert 26
Heidegger, Martin 46, 50-55, 57, 58, 63, 64, 69, 74, 103, 104, 116
Herder, Johann Gottfried 24
Hitchcock, Henry Russell 30
Hochman, Elaine 123
Husserl, Edmund 109
Ibsen, Henrik 101, 102
Idealism 50
Irigaray, Luce 109
Jencks, Charles 45
Joedicke, Jürgen 32
Kafka, Franz 45
Kahn, Louis 56
Kandinsky, Vasily Vasilyevich 112
Kant, Immanuel 17, 51, 65, 91
Keillor, Garrison 45
Khrushchev, Nikita 39
Kipnis, Jeffrey 73, 94-99, 114, 117
Koffka, Kurt 78
Krier, Leon 135

Kuhn, Thomas 47, 49
Lamprecht, Karl 24, 25
Le Corbusier 21-23, 28, 29, 37, 38, 29, 41, 113, 123-126
Leibniz, Gottfried Wilhelm 16, 106, 109-112
Lempedusa, Tomasi 107
Liebeskind, Daniel 89
Lobachevsky, Nikolai 63
Loos, Adolf 20, 38, 39, 123
Lynn, Greg 34, 109-112
Maillart, Robert 35
Mallgrave, Harry Francis 124
Mann, Thomas 51, 71, 100, 101
Marcel Gabriel 51
Marx, Karl 64
Maxentius, Marcus Aurelius Valerius 120
McKim, Mead and White 22, 29, 32
Mendelsohn, Erich 27, 40, 123
Meyer, Hannes 18, 116
Mies van der Rohe, Ludwig 10, 17, 18, 20-22, 27, 28, 32, 33, 37, 39, 40, 46, 57, 80, 103, 122-126
Minkowski, Hermann 35
Modernism 10, 16-44, 122-131
Muthesius, Hermann 18
Nitzsche, Friedrich 55
Norberg-Schulz, Christian 46-55, 58, 60, 65-70, 96, 119
Object Oriented Ontology 14, 115-119
Oud, Jacobus 21
Palladio, Andrea 17, 32, 42, 61, 84, 85, 96
Pallasmaa, Juhani 56, 59, 60, 67, 70, 132
Palmerston, Henry John Temple 129
Pérez-Gómez, Alberto 49, 70, 95
Pevsner, Nikolaus 28, 35, 36, 37, 129
Phenomenology 13, 45-70
Picasso, Pablo 35
Pikionis, Dimitris 63
Plato 86
Ponti, Giovanni 32
Pope, John Russell 22, 29, 30, 31, 33
Porphyrios, Demetri 135
Rajchman, John 75, 107, 108
Richards, J. M. 32

Riegl, Alois 25
Riemann, Georg 63
Rorty, Richard 102
Rowe, Collin 75
Sansovino, Jacopo 33, 85
Sant' Elia, Antonio 20, 23, 123
Schildt, Göran 123
Schmarsow, August 63
Schumacher, Patrik 40, 67, 104, 112-115, 127
Scott, Geoffrey 16, 17, 20, 42, 43, 133
Scott, George Gilbert 129
Sedlmayr, Hans 36, 78
Smith, Thomas Gordon 135
Sokal, Alan 15, 109
Speaks, Michael 107
Speer, Albert 29, 41
Spengler, Oswald 25, 26, 27
Spinoza, Baruch 26, 106
Stalin, Joseph Vissarionovich 41
Stone, Edward Durrell 21
Sykes, Krista 106, 108
Taut, Bruno 27, 123
Terjei Vasaas 60
Terry, Quinlan 135
Theodoric, Flavius 130
Troost, Paul Ludwig 32
Tschumi, Bernard 73, 82-84, 90-92, 113, 129
Utzon, Jørn 58
Venturi, Robert 75
Vermeer, Johannes 26
Vesely, Dalibor 49, 68
Vignola, Jacopo Barozzi 127
Vitruvius, Marcus Pollio 84
Wagner, Otto 18, 39, 123
Walton, Kendall 105
Watkin, David 35
Wigley, Mark 82, 83, 87, 88, 91, 92, 103
Wolfe, Thomas 11, 130
Worringer, Wilhelm 26
Wright, Frank Lloyd 21, 31, 41, 123, 124, 126
Zangwill, Nick 105
Zeitgeist 24, 25, 28, 34, 77
Zevi, Bruno 40
Zholtovsky, Ivan Vladislavovich 29